100 STIR-FRIES
AND QUICK CURRIES

100 STIR-FRIES
AND QUICK CURRIES

SPICY, FAST AND AROMATIC DISHES FROM ASIA AND THE FAR EAST,
SHOWN STEP-BY-STEP IN MORE THAN 300 SIZZLING PHOTOGRAPHS

CONSULTANT EDITOR: JENNI FLEETWOOD

southwater

This edition is published by Southwater, an imprint of
Anness Publishing Ltd, Hermes House, 88–89 Blackfriars Road,
London SE1 8HA; tel. 020 7401 2077; fax 020 7633 9499
www.southwaterbooks.com; www.annesspublishing.com

If you like the images in this book and would like to investigate using
them for publishing, promotions or advertising, please visit our website
www.practicalpictures.com for more information.

UK agent: The Manning Partnership Ltd; tel. 01225 478444;
fax 01225 478440; sales@manning-partnership.co.uk
UK distributor: Grantham Book Services Ltd; tel. 01476 541080;
fax 01476 541061; orders@gbs.tbs-ltd.co.uk
North American agent/distributor: National Book Network;
tel. 301 459 3366; fax 301 429 5746; www.nbnbooks.com
Australian agent/distributor: Pan Macmillan Australia; tel. 1300 135
113; fax 1300 135 103; customer.service@macmillan.com.au
New Zealand agent/distributor: David Bateman Ltd; tel. (09) 415 7664;
fax (09) 415 8892

Publisher: Joanna Lorenz
Editorial Director: Helen Sudell
Executive Editor: Joanne Rippin
Photographs: Nicki Dowey, Gus Filgate, Craig Robertson
Additional Recipes: Yasuko Fukuoka, Deh-Ta Hsiung
Designer: Adelle Morris
Production Controller: Wendy Lawson
Editorial Reader: Alison Bolus

© Anness Publishing Ltd 2007, 2008

ETHICAL TRADING POLICY
Because of our ongoing ecological investment programme, you, as our
customer, can have the pleasure and reassurance of knowing that a
tree is being cultivated on your behalf to naturally replace the materials
used to make the book you are holding. For further information about
this scheme, go to www.annesspublishing.com/trees.

NOTES
Bracketed terms are intended for American readers.
For all recipes, quantities are given in both metric and imperial
measures and, where appropriate, in standard cups and spoons.
Follow one set of measures, but not a mixture, because they are not
interchangeable.
Standard spoon and cup measures are level. 1 tsp = 5ml, 1 tbsp =
15ml, 1 cup = 250ml/8fl oz.
Australian standard tablespoons are 20ml. Australian readers should
use 3 tsp in place of 1 tbsp for measuring small quantities.
American pints are 16fl oz/2 cups. American readers should use 20fl
oz/2.5 cups in place of 1 pint when measuring liquids.
Electric oven temperatures in this book are for conventional ovens.
When using a fan oven, the temperature will probably need to be
reduced by about 10–20°C/20–40°F. Since ovens vary, you should
check with your manufacturer's instruction book for guidance.
The nutritional analysis given for each recipe is calculated per portion
(i.e. serving or item), unless otherwise stated. If the recipe gives a
range, such as Serves 4–6, then the nutritional analysis will be for the
smaller portion size, i.e. 6 servings. Measurements for sodium do not
include salt added to taste.

CONTENTS

INTRODUCTION

The wok is a wonderful invention, as suited to contemporary cooking as it is to recreating classic recipes from its country of origin. There should be one in every kitchen, as it proves its worth over and over again.

Wok sales have rocketed in recent years. In the 1960s and 70s, a wok was something of a novelty, often bought in a burst of enthusiasm after a visit to a Chinese restaurant, then left to rust at the back of a kitchen cupboard. Fortunately, there were enough fans of this excellent pan to spread the word, and the wok gradually gained ground.

This book contains recipes that can be created with speed and enjoyment, using fresh ingredients and a single pan. They are therefore ideal for busy cooks who want to eat well and healthily without spending hours in the kitchen. There are some important things to remember when you are cooking stir fries or curries in the wok.

Proper preparation is vital, especially when you are stir-frying, which is so fast it is essential to have everything ready before you begin. That means slicing vegetables, meat or fish to the size required, having sauces handy and making sure that implements needed are within reach. Asian cooks take a great deal of care over the preparation of ingredients. There is an aesthetic reason for this – food must look as well as taste good – but careful cutting also serves a practical purpose. Cutting all

Below: Squash and pumpkin benefit from slow simmering in the wok to develop their sweet flavour.

Above: The wok is a great tool for frying small pieces, or portions, of meat.

the pieces to a uniform size means they cook quickly and evenly.

When stir-frying it is important to remember that the wok must be preheated. If the wok is hot when you add the oil, it will coat the surface with a thin film, preventing the food from sticking. The best way to do this is to add a trickle of oil, necklace-fashion, around the inner rim so that it runs down evenly. You don't need much.

Below: Tofu is a staple ingredient in China and Japan, and is used in many different types of wok recipes.

When stir-frying meat, don't overload the wok or you will bring down the temperature. Add a few pieces at a time, sear them for a few seconds, flip them over and sear them on the other side, then push them away from the centre, where the heat is concentrated, or remove them from the pan, and add more meat to the well.

Vegetables are usually added after the meat and you need to start with varieties that take the longest to cook, such as carrots and sweet (bell) peppers. Vegetables that need very little cooking, such as mooli (daikon) and mushrooms should be added next, with leafy vegetables tossed in right at the end. Keep the food on the move all the time, using a flipping and turning movement with a spatula.

When making dishes such as curries they will need a slower, longer cooking time to develop flavours and texture. Initially, ingredients will probably be fried quickly as in a stir-fry, after which other ingredients and liquid are added, and the heat reduced to a simmer. Because of its shape, the wok is ideal for rapid reduction of liquids, if you are cooking for a longer time, therefore, you need to keep a close eye on the level of liquid, and top up if necessary.

Right: The use of the wok has developed from its origins in Asia and the Far East, into a pan used all over the world for many different dishes.

Below: Vegetables make perfect ingredients for stir fries, the fast cooking means that vitamins are retained.

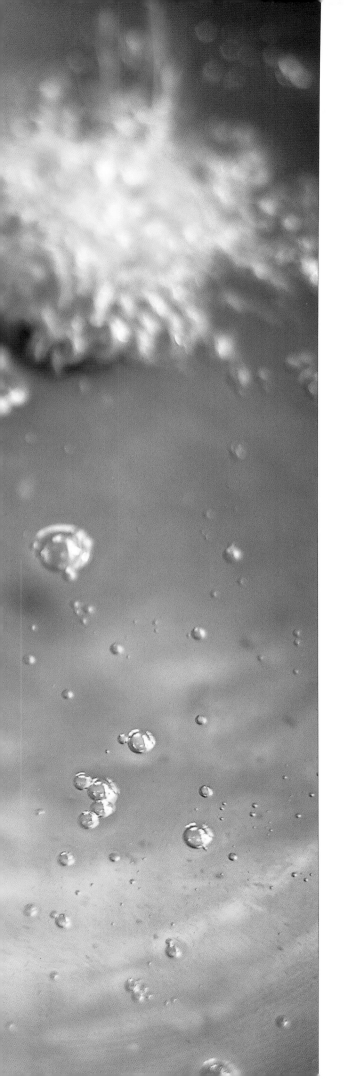

SOUPS AND APPETIZERS

For swift soups, such as those based on ready-made stock or canned bouillon, a wok is ideal. The large surface area makes for rapid evaporation, though, so you need to keep an eye on liquid levels and top up if necessary. This is an area where an electric wok can work wonders. Any preliminary cooking can be done at a high heat, and the thermostat can then be turned down so the soup simmers well. This chapter includes delicious, and nutritious Hot and Sour Soup, and Tofu and Beansprout soup, as well as more complex and robust main course soups such as Tokyo-style Ramen Noodles in Soup. The chapter ends with some delicious, crispy fried appetizers to stimulate the appetite.

TOFU AND BEANSPROUT SOUP

THIS LIGHT AND REFRESHING SOUP IS VERY QUICK AND EASY TO MAKE IN THE WOK. THE AROMATIC SPICY BROTH IS SIMMERED BRIEFLY AND THEN THE TOFU, BEANSPROUTS AND NOODLES ARE QUICKLY COOKED. USE FIRM TOFU BECAUSE THE SOFTER VARIETY WILL DISINTEGRATE DURING COOKING.

SERVES FOUR

INGREDIENTS

150g/5oz dried thick rice noodles
1 litre/1¾ pints/4 cups
  vegetable stock
1 fresh red chilli, seeded and finely
  sliced
15ml/1 tbsp light soy sauce
juice of 1 small lime
10ml/2 tsp palm sugar (jaggery)
5ml/1 tsp thinly sliced garlic
5ml/1 tsp finely chopped
  fresh root ginger
200g/7oz firm tofu
90g/3½oz mung beansprouts
30ml/2 tbsp chopped fresh mint
15ml/1 tbsp chopped fresh
  coriander (cilantro)
15ml/1 tbsp chopped fresh
  sweet basil
50g/2oz/½ cup roasted peanuts,
  roughly chopped
spring onion (scallion) slivers and red
  (bell) pepper slivers, to garnish

1 Place the noodles in a bowl and pour over enough boiling water to cover. Soak for 10–15 minutes, until soft. Drain, rinse and set aside.

2 Place the stock, red chilli, soy sauce, lime juice, palm sugar, garlic and ginger in a wok over a high heat. Bring to the boil, cover, reduce to a low heat and simmer for 10–12 minutes.

3 Meanwhile, cut the firm tofu into neat cubes, using a sharp knife or cleaver. Add the tofu to the soup.

4 Add the drained noodles and beansprouts to the soup and cook gently for just 2–3 minutes. Remove from the heat and stir in the herbs. Ladle the soup into bowls and sprinkle over the peanuts. Garnish with spring onion and red pepper slivers if liked.

COOK'S TIP
Palm sugar is dense and crumbly and needs to be grated or melted before use. Soft brown sugar can be substituted.

Energy 266Kcal/1108kJ; Protein 10.5g; Carbohydrate 35.1g, of which sugars 3g; Fat 8.8g, of which saturates 1.4g; Cholesterol 0mg; Calcium 321mg; Fibre 2.4g; Sodium 115mg.

HOT AND SOUR SOUP

ONE OF CHINA'S MOST POPULAR SOUPS, THIS IS FAMED FOR ITS CLEVER BALANCE OF FLAVOURS. THE "HOT" COMES FROM PEPPER; THE "SOUR" FROM VINEGAR. SIMILAR SOUPS ARE FOUND THROUGHOUT ASIA, SOME RELYING ON CHILLIES AND LIME JUICE TO PROVIDE THE ESSENTIAL FLAVOUR CONTRAST.

SERVES SIX

INGREDIENTS

4–6 Chinese dried mushrooms
2–3 small pieces of cloud ear (wood
  ear) mushrooms and a few golden
  needles (lily buds) (optional)
115g/4oz pork fillet (tenderloin), cut
  into fine strips
45ml/3 tbsp cornflour (cornstarch)
150ml/¼ pint/⅔ cup water
15–30ml/1–2 tbsp sunflower oil
1 small onion, finely chopped
1.5 litres/2½ pints/6¼ cups good
  quality beef or chicken stock, or
  2 × 300g/11oz cans consommé made
  up to the full quantity with water
150g/5oz fresh firm tofu, diced
60ml/4 tbsp rice vinegar
15ml/1 tbsp light soy sauce
1 egg, beaten
5 ml/1 tsp sesame oil
salt and ground white or black pepper
2–3 spring onions (scallions),
  shredded, to garnish

1 Place the dried mushrooms in a bowl, with the pieces of cloud ear and the golden needles, if using. Add sufficient warm water to cover and leave to soak for about 30 minutes.

3 Lightly dust the strips of pork fillet with some of the cornflour; mix the remaining cornflour to a smooth paste with the measured water.

5 Discard the golden needles, lower the heat and stir in the cornflour paste to thicken. Add the tofu, vinegar, soy sauce, and salt and pepper.

2 Drain the mushrooms, reserving the soaking water. Cut off and discard the mushroom stems and slice the caps finely. Trim away any tough stem from the wood ears, then chop them finely. Using kitchen string, tie the golden needles into a bundle.

4 Heat the oil in a wok and fry the onion until soft. Increase the heat and fry the pork until it changes colour. Add the stock or consommé, mushrooms, soaking water, and cloud ears and golden needles, if using. Bring to the boil, then simmer for 15 minutes.

6 Bring the soup to just below boiling point, then drizzle in the beaten egg by letting it drop from a whisk (or to be authentic, the fingertips) so that it forms threads in the soup. Stir in the sesame oil and serve at once, garnished with spring onion shreds.

Energy 103Kcal/429kJ; Protein 7.3g; Carbohydrate 7.3g, of which sugars 0.3g; Fat 5.1g, of which saturates 1g; Cholesterol 44mg; Calcium 135mg; Fibre 0g; Sodium 208mg.

BALINESE VEGETABLE SOUP

THE BALINESE BASE THIS POPULAR SOUP ON BEANS, BUT ANY SEASONAL VEGETABLES CAN BE ADDED OR SUBSTITUTED. THE RECIPE ALSO INCLUDES SHRIMP PASTE, WHICH IS KNOWN LOCALLY AS TERASI.

2 Finely grind the chopped garlic, macadamia nuts or almonds, shrimp paste and the coriander seeds to a paste using a pestle and mortar or in a food processor.

3 Heat a wok, add the oil, and when it is hot, fry the onion until transparent. Remove with a slotted spoon. Add the nut paste to the wok and fry it for 2 minutes without allowing it to brown.

4 Pour in the reserved vegetable water. Spoon off 45–60ml/3–4 tbsp of the cream from the top of the coconut milk and set it aside. Add the remaining coconut milk to the wok, bring to the boil and add the bay leaves. Cook, uncovered, for 15–20 minutes.

SERVES EIGHT

INGREDIENTS
  225g/8oz green beans
  1.2 litres/2 pints/5 cups lightly
    salted water
  1 garlic clove, roughly chopped
  2 macadamia nuts or 4 almonds,
    finely chopped
  1cm/½in cube shrimp paste
  10–15ml/2–3 tsp coriander seeds,
    dry-fried
  30ml/2 tbsp vegetable oil
  1 onion, finely sliced
  400ml/14fl oz can coconut milk
  2 bay leaves
  225g/8oz/4 cups beansprouts
  8 thin lemon wedges
  30ml/2 tbsp lemon juice
  salt and ground black pepper

1 Trim the beans and cut into small pieces. Bring the lightly salted water to the boil, add the beans to the pan and cook for 3–4 minutes. Drain, reserving the cooking water. Set the beans aside.

COOK'S TIP
Dry-fry the coriander seeds for about 2 minutes until the aroma is released.

5 Just before serving, reserve a few beans, fried onions and beansprouts for garnish and stir the rest into the soup. Add the lemon wedges, reserved coconut cream, lemon juice and seasoning; warm through, stirring well.

6 Pour into individual soup bowls and serve, garnished with the reserved beans, onion and beansprouts.

Energy 63Kcal/263kJ; Protein 2.2g; Carbohydrate 5.2g, of which sugars 4.2g; Fat 3.9g, of which saturates 0.5g; Cholesterol 3mg; Calcium 43mg; Fibre 1.2g; Sodium 84mg.

CRISPY WONTON SOUP

THE FRESHLY COOKED CRISPY WONTONS ARE SUPPOSED TO SIZZLE AND "SING" AS THE HOT FAT HITS THE SOUP, SO ADD THEM JUST BEFORE YOU TAKE THE BOWLS TO THE TABLE.

SERVES SIX

INGREDIENTS

    2 cloud ear (wood ear) mushrooms,
      soaked for 30 minutes in warm
      water to cover
    1.2 litres/2 pints/5 cups
      home-made chicken stock
    2.5cm/1in piece fresh root ginger,
      peeled and grated
    4 spring onions (scallions), chopped
    2 rich-green inner spring greens
      leaves, finely shredded
    50g/2oz drained canned bamboo
      shoots, sliced
    25ml/1½ tbsp dark soy sauce
    2.5ml/½ tsp sesame oil
    salt and ground black pepper
For the filled wontons
    5ml/1 tsp sesame oil
    ½ small onion, finely chopped
    10 drained canned water
      chestnuts, finely chopped
    115g/4oz finely minced (ground) pork
    24 wonton wrappers
    groundnut (peanut) oil, for frying

2 Place the wonton wrappers under a slightly dampened dish towel so that they do not dry out. Next, dampen the edges of a wonton wrapper. Place about 5ml/1 tsp of the filling in the centre of the wrapper. Gather it up like a purse and twist the top or roll up as you would a baby spring roll. Fill the remaining wontons in the same way.

3 To make the soup, drain the cloud ears, discarding the soaking liquid. Trim away any rough stems, then slice thinly.

4 Bring the stock to the boil, add the ginger and the spring onions and simmer for 3 minutes. Add the cloud ears, spring greens, bamboo shoots and soy sauce. Simmer for 10 minutes, then stir in the sesame oil. Season with salt and pepper, cover and keep hot.

5 Heat the oil in a wok to 190°C/375°F and fry the wontons for 3–4 minutes or until they are crisp and golden. Ladle the soup into warmed bowls, share the wontons among them, and serve.

1 Make the filled wontons. Heat the sesame oil in a small pan, add the onion, water chestnuts and pork and fry, stirring occasionally, until the meat is no longer pink. Tip into a bowl, season to taste and leave to cool.

COOK'S TIP
The wontons can be filled up to two hours ahead. Place them in a single layer on a baking sheet dusted with cornflour, to prevent them from sticking, and leave in a cool place.

Energy 108Kcal/456kJ; Protein 6.3g; Carbohydrate 14.4g, of which sugars 1.4g; Fat 3.3g, of which saturates 0.9g; Cholesterol 13mg; Calcium 69mg; Fibre 1.4g; Sodium 249mg.

TOKYO-STYLE RAMEN NOODLES IN SOUP

A WOK IS ALL YOU NEED TO MAKE THIS MULTI-LAYERED JAPANESE SOUP. THERE ARE MANY REGIONAL AND LOCAL VARIATIONS OF RAMEN, THIS IS A LEGENDARY TOKYO VERSION.

SERVES FOUR

INGREDIENTS
 250g/9oz dried ramen noodles
For the soup stock
 4 spring onions (scallions)
 7.5cm/3in fresh root ginger, quartered
 raw bones from 2 chickens, washed
 1 large onion, quartered
 4 garlic cloves, peeled
 1 large carrot, roughly chopped
 1 egg shell
 120ml/4fl oz/½ cup sake
 about 60ml/4 tbsp shoyu
 2.5ml/½ tsp salt
For the *cha-shu* (pot-roast pork)
 500g/1¼lb pork shoulder, boned
 30ml/2 tbsp vegetable oil
 2 spring onions (scallions), chopped
 2.5cm/1in fresh root ginger, peeled
  and sliced
 15ml/1 tbsp sake
 45ml/3 tbsp shoyu
 15ml/1 tbsp caster (superfine) sugar
For the toppings
 2 hard-boiled eggs
 150g/5oz pickled bamboo shoots,
  soaked for 30 minutes and drained
 ½ nori sheet, broken into pieces
 2 spring onions (scallions), chopped
 ground white pepper
 sesame oil or chilli oil

1 To make the soup stock, bruise the spring onions and ginger by hitting with the side of a large knife or a rolling pin. Pour 1.5 litres/2½ pints/6¼ cups water into a wok and bring to the boil. Add the chicken bones and boil until the colour of the meat changes. Discard the water and wash the bones under water.

2 Wash the wok, bring another 2 litres/3½ pints/9 cups water to the boil and add the bones and the other soup stock ingredients, except for the shoyu and salt. Reduce the heat to low, and simmer for up to 2 hours until the water has reduced by half, skimming off any scum. Strain into a bowl through a sieve lined with muslin (cheesecloth).

3 Make the *cha-shu*. Roll the meat up tightly, to 8cm/3½in in diameter, and tie it with kitchen string.

4 Wash the wok and dry over a high heat. Heat the oil to smoking point in the wok and add the chopped spring onions and ginger. Cook briefly, then add the meat. Turn often to brown the outside evenly.

5 Sprinkle with sake and add 400ml/14fl oz/1⅔ cups water, the shoyu and sugar. Boil, then reduce the heat to low and cover. Cook for 25–30 minutes, turning every 5 minutes. Remove from the heat.

6 Slice the pork into 12 fine slices. Use any leftover pork for another recipe.

7 Shell and halve the boiled eggs, and sprinkle some salt on to the yolks.

8 Pour 1 litre/1¾ pints/4 cups soup stock from the bowl into a large pan. Boil and add the shoyu and salt. Check the seasoning; add more shoyu if required.

9 Wash the wok again and bring 2 litres/3½ pints/9 cups water to the boil. Cook the ramen noodles according to the packet instructions until just soft. Stir constantly to prevent sticking. If the water bubbles up, pour in 50ml/2fl oz/¼ cup cold water. Drain well and divide among four bowls.

10 Pour the soup over the noodles to cover. Arrange half a boiled egg, pork slices, pickled bamboo shoots, and nori on top, and sprinkle with spring onions. Serve with pepper and sesame or chilli oil. Season to taste with a little salt, if you like.

COOK'S TIP
The cooked pork could be finely chopped and minced and used as part of the filling for spring rolls.

Energy 521Kcal/2193kJ; Protein 38.9g; Carbohydrate 55.6g, of which sugars 8.7g; Fat 17.5g, of which saturates 3.2g; Cholesterol 174mg; Calcium 57mg; Fibre 3g; Sodium 843mg.

CHINESE LEAF, MEATBALL AND NOODLE BROTH

THIS WONDERFULLY FRAGRANT COMBINATION OF SPICED MEATBALLS, NOODLES AND VEGETABLES COOKED SLOWLY IN A RICHLY FLAVOURED BROTH MAKES FOR A VERY HEARTY, WARMING SOUP. SERVE IT AS A MAIN COURSE ON A COLD WINTER EVENING, DRIZZLED WITH CHILLI OIL FOR A LITTLE EXTRA HEAT. SAVOY CABBAGE CAN BE SUBSTITUTED FOR CHINESE LEAVES.

SERVES FOUR

INGREDIENTS

10 dried shiitake mushrooms
90g/3½oz bean thread noodles
675g/1½lb minced (ground) beef
10ml/2 tsp finely grated garlic
10ml/2 tsp finely grated fresh
  root ginger
1 fresh red chilli, seeded and
  chopped
6 spring onions (scallions),
  finely sliced
1 egg white
15ml/1 tbsp cornflour (cornstarch)
15ml/1 tbsp Chinese rice wine
30ml/2 tbsp sunflower oil
1.5 litres/2½ pints/6¼ cups chicken
  or beef stock
50ml/2fl oz/¼ cup light soy sauce
5ml/1 tsp sugar
150g/5oz enoki mushrooms, trimmed
200g/7oz Chinese leaves (Chinese
  cabbage) very thinly sliced
salt and ground black pepper
sesame oil and chilli oil,
  to drizzle (optional)

1 Place the dried mushrooms in a bowl and pour over 250ml/8fl oz/1 cup boiling water. Leave to soak for 30 minutes and then squeeze dry, reserving the soaking liquid.

2 Cut the stems from the mushrooms and discard, then thickly slice the caps and set aside.

3 Put the noodles in a large bowl and pour over boiling water to cover. Leave to soak for 3–4 minutes, then drain, rinse and set aside.

4 Place the beef, garlic, ginger, chilli, spring onions, egg white, cornflour, rice wine and seasoning in a food processor. Process to combine well.

5 Transfer the mixture to a bowl and divide into 30 portions, then shape each one into a ball.

6 Heat a wok over a high heat and add the oil. Fry the meatballs, in batches, for 2–3 minutes on each side until lightly browned. Remove with a slotted spoon and drain on kitchen paper.

7 Wipe out the wok and place over a high heat. Add the stock, soy sauce, sugar and shiitake mushrooms with the reserved soaking liquid and bring to the boil.

8 Add the meatballs to the boiling stock, reduce the heat and cook gently for 20–25 minutes.

9 Add the noodles, enoki mushrooms and cabbage to the wok and cook gently for 4–5 minutes. Serve ladled into wide shallow bowls. Drizzle with sesame oil and chilli oil, if liked.

Energy 548Kcal/2279kJ; Protein 36.8g; Carbohydrate 24.9g, of which sugars 3g; Fat 33.3g, of which saturates 12.4g; Cholesterol 101mg; Calcium 52mg; Fibre 1.7g; Sodium 161mg.

THAI AUBERGINE AND PEPPER TEMPURA WITH SWEET CHILLI DIP

THESE CRUNCHY VEGETABLES IN A BEAUTIFULLY LIGHT BATTER ARE QUICK AND EASY TO MAKE AND TASTE VERY GOOD WITH THE PIQUANT DIP. ALTHOUGH TEMPURA IS A SIGNATURE DISH OF JAPANESE CUISINE, IT HAS NOW BECOME POPULAR THROUGHOUT ASIA, WITH EACH COUNTRY ADDING ITS OWN CHARACTERISTIC TOUCH — IN THE CASE OF THAILAND, THIS CHILLI-FLAVOURED SAUCE.

SERVES FOUR

INGREDIENTS

2 aubergines (eggplants)
2 red (bell) peppers
vegetable oil, for deep-frying
For the tempura batter
    250g/9oz/2¼ cups plain
      (all-purpose) flour
    2 egg yolks
    500ml/17fl oz/2¼ cups iced water
    5ml/1 tsp salt
For the dip
    150ml/¼ pint/⅔ cup water
    10ml/2 tsp granulated sugar
    1 fresh red chilli, seeded and
      finely chopped
    1 garlic clove, crushed
    juice of ½ lime
    5ml/1 tsp rice vinegar
    35ml/2½ tbsp Thai fish sauce
    ½ small carrot, finely grated

1 Using a sharp knife or a mandolin, slice the aubergines into thin batons. Halve, seed and slice the red peppers thinly.

2 Make the dip. Mix together all the ingredients in a bowl and stir until the sugar has dissolved. Cover with clear film (plastic wrap) and set aside.

VARIATIONS
Tempura batter is also good with pieces of fish or whole shellfish, such as large prawns (jumbo shrimp) or baby squid, as well as with a variety of vegetables.

3 Make the tempura batter. Set aside 30ml/2 tbsp of the flour. Put the egg yolks in a large bowl and beat in the iced water. Tip in the remaining flour with the salt and stir briefly together – the mixture should resemble thick pancake batter but be lumpy and not properly mixed. If it is too thick, add a little more iced water. Do not leave the batter to stand; use it immediately.

4 Pour the oil for deep-frying into a wok or deep-fryer and heat to 190°C/375°F or until a cube of bread, added to the oil, browns in about 40 seconds.

5 Pick up a small, haphazard handful of aubergine batons and pepper slices, dust it with the reserved flour, then dip it into the batter. Immediately drop the batter-coated vegetables into the hot oil, taking care as the oil will froth up furiously. Repeat to make two or three more fritters, but do not cook any more than this at one time, or the oil may overflow.

6 Cook the fritters for 3–4 minutes, until they are golden and crisp all over, then lift them out with a metal basket or slotted spoon. Drain thoroughly on kitchen paper and keep hot.

7 Repeat until all the vegetables have been coated in batter and cooked. Serve immediately, with the dip.

Energy 404Kcal/1699kJ; Protein 9.4g; Carbohydrate 61g, of which sugars 12.5g; Fat 15.4g, of which saturates 2.4g; Cholesterol 101mg; Calcium 124mg; Fibre 5.8g; Sodium 15mg.

STIR-FRIED CLAMS WITH ORANGE AND GARLIC

ZESTY ORANGE JUICE COMBINED WITH PUNGENT GARLIC AND SHALLOTS MAKE SURPRISINGLY GOOD PARTNERS FOR THE SWEET-TASTING SHELLFISH. FRESH, PLUMP CLAMS WILL RELEASE PLENTY OF JUICES WHILE THEY ARE COOKING, SO SERVE WITH SOME BREAD TO MOP UP THE DELICIOUS SAUCE.

SERVES FOUR

INGREDIENTS

1kg/2¼lb fresh clams
15ml/1 tbsp sunflower oil
30ml/2 tbsp finely chopped garlic
4 shallots, finely chopped
105ml/7 tbsp vegetable or fish stock
finely grated rind and
  juice of 1 orange
salt and ground black pepper
a large handful of roughly
  chopped flat leaf parsley

COOK'S TIP
To avoid the risk of food poisoning, it is essential that the clams are live before cooking. Tap any open clams with the back of a knife. Any that do not close are dead and so must be discarded; and any that remain closed after cooking should also be thrown away.

1 Wash and scrub the clams under cold running water. Check carefully and discard any that are open and do not close when tapped lightly.

2 Heat a wok over a high heat and add the sunflower oil. When hot, add the garlic, shallots and clams and stir-fry for 4–5 minutes.

3 Add the stock and orange rind and juice to the wok and season well. Cover and cook for 3–4 minutes, or until all the clams have opened. (Discard any unopened clams.)

4 Stir the chopped flat leaf parsley into the clams, then remove from the heat and serve immediately.

Energy 142Kcal/596kJ; Protein 21.4g; Carbohydrate 5.9g, of which sugars 1.6g; Fat 3.8g, of which saturates 0.6g; Cholesterol 84mg; Calcium 121mg; Fibre 1.2g; Sodium 1506mg.

PARCHMENT-WRAPPED PRAWNS

THESE SUCCULENT PINK PRAWNS COATED IN A FRAGRANT SPICE PASTE MAKE THE PERFECT DISH FOR INFORMAL ENTERTAINING. SERVE THE PRAWNS IN THEIR PAPER PARCELS AND ALLOW YOUR GUESTS TO UNWRAP THEM AT THE TABLE AND ENJOY THE AROMA OF THAI SPICES AS THE PARCEL IS OPENED.

SERVES FOUR

INGREDIENTS

2 lemon grass stalks, very
  finely chopped
5ml/1 tsp galangal, very finely
  chopped
4 garlic cloves, finely chopped
finely grated rind and juice
  of 1 lime
4 spring onions (scallions), chopped
10ml/2 tsp palm sugar
15ml/1 tbsp soy sauce
5ml/1 tsp Thai fish sauce
5ml/1 tsp chilli oil
45ml/3 tbsp chopped fresh coriander
  (cilantro) leaves
30ml/2 tbsp chopped fresh Thai
  basil leaves
1kg/2¼lb raw tiger prawns (jumbo
  shrimp), heads and shells removed
  but with tails left on
basil leaves and lime wedges,
  to garnish

1 Place the lemon grass, galangal, garlic, lime rind and juice and spring onions in a food processor or blender. Blend in short bursts until the mixture forms a coarse paste.

2 Transfer the paste to a large bowl and stir in the palm sugar, soy sauce, fish sauce, chilli oil and chopped herbs.

3 Add the prawns to the paste and toss to coat evenly. Cover and marinate in the refrigerator for 30 minutes–1 hour.

4 Cut out eight 20cm/8in squares of baking parchment. Place one-eighth of the prawn mixture in the centre of each one, then fold over the edges and twist together to make a sealed parcel.

5 Place the parcels in a large bamboo steamer, cover and steam over a wok of simmering water for 10 minutes, or until the prawns are just cooked through. Serve immediately garnished with basil leaves and lime wedges.

Energy 169Kcal/713kJ; Protein 35.4g; Carbohydrate 2.4g, of which sugars 2.4g; Fat 2g, of which saturates 0.3g; Cholesterol 390mg; Calcium 163mg; Fibre 0.2g; Sodium 381mg.

DIPS AND GARNISHES

There are various sauces that combine the flavours of wok cooking, which can be used for dipping, but also as stir-in sauces for quickly stir-fried vegetables.

Thai Red Curry Dip

This tastes good with mini spring rolls, or can be tossed with rice noodles for a simple accompaniment.

SERVES 4

    200ml/7fl oz/scant 1 cup coconut
      cream
    10–15ml/2–3 tsp Thai red curry
      paste
    4 spring onions (scallions), plus
      extra, thinly sliced, to garnish
    30ml/2 tbsp chopped fresh coriander
      (cilantro)
    1 fresh red chilli, seeded and thinly
      sliced in rings
    5ml/1 tsp soy sauce
    juice of 1 lime
    sugar, to taste
    25g/1oz/3 tbsp dry-roasted peanuts,
      finely chopped
    salt and ground black pepper

Pour the coconut cream into a small bowl and stir in the curry paste. Trim the spring onions, slice them diagonally, then stir into the coconut cream with the coriander, chilli, soy sauce and lime juice. Add enough sugar to give a sweet-sour flavour and season with salt and pepper. Spoon into a serving bowl and top with the peanuts and thinly sliced spring onion.

Wasabi and Soy Dip

Try this with any kind of tempura. The combination works extremely well, especially if you add a squeeze of lime just before dipping.

SERVES 4

    175ml/6fl oz/³/4 cup soy sauce or
      shoyu
    10ml/2 tsp wasabi paste
    2 spring onions (scallions), diagonally
      sliced
    1 fresh red chilli, seeded and thinly
      sliced in rings (optional)

Mix the soy sauce or shoyu with the wasabi paste in a bowl. Float the spring onion slices on top. The chilli slices can be added or left out, depending on how spicy you want the dip to be. Top with just one or two rings for colour.

Sweet Chilli Sauce

This sweet, spicy sauce has a wonderfully aromatic flavour and lovely translucent red colour. It can be used both for flavouring and as a dipping sauce. Any remaining sauce can be stored in the refrigerator in an airtight container for 1–2 weeks.

SERVES 4

    6 large red chillies
    60ml/4 tbsp white vinegar
    250g/9oz caster (superfine) sugar
    5ml/1tsp salt
    4 garlic cloves, chopped

Place the chillies in a food processor. Add the vinegar, sugar, salt and garlic. Blend until smooth, transfer to a pan and cook over a medium heat until thickened. Leave to cool and then transfer to a bowl.

Tamarind Sauce

This sweet, tangy dipping sauce has a fruity flavour and is perfect served with spicy deep-fried snacks. The quantities here are suitable for one serving, but if there is any left over, transfer into an airtight container and store in the refrigerator for 1–2 weeks.

MAKES 1 SMALL JAR
90ml/6 tbsp tamarind paste
90ml/6 tbsp water
45ml/3 tbsp caster (superfine) sugar

Place all the ingredients in a small pan and bring the mixture to the boil. Reduce the heat and cook gently for 3–4 minutes, stirring occasionally. Remove the pan from the heat and transfer to a small bowl. Leave to cool before serving.

Wasabi paste

This bright green paste packs a whopping punch. It is made from a Japanese herb and tastes like a cross between hot mustard and horseradish. A little goes a long way to flavour dips and sauces. Try mixing it with mayonnaise for a delicious dip to serve with steamed asparagus. The most convenient way to buy wasabi is in a tube. If you use powdered wasabi, mix it in an egg cup with the same volume of tepid water, then stand the egg cup upside down for 10 minutes to allow the flavour to develop without letting the wasabi dry out.

Ginger and Hoisin Dip

Chunky and bursting with flavour, this dip is delicious with prawn (shrimp) crackers. The dip can be stored in the refrigerator for up to 1 week.

SERVES 4
60ml/4 tbsp hoisin sauce
120ml/4fl oz/$\frac{1}{2}$ cup passata (bottled strained tomatoes)
4 spring onions (scallions), thinly sliced
4cm/1$\frac{1}{2}$in piece fresh root ginger, peeled and finely chopped
2 fresh red chillies, seeded and cut into fine strips
2 garlic cloves, crushed
few drops of roasted sesame oil

Mix the hoisin and passata in a bowl. Stir in the spring onions, ginger, chillies and crushed garlic. Add the sesame oil, mix well and serve.

GREAT GARNISHES

Thai cooks enjoy garnishing their dishes with beautifully cut vegetables. Here are some suggestions for easy finishing touches that look fabulous. A cucumber frill makes a lovely garnish for duck, steamed salmon, a stir-fry or salad.

Cut a cucumber in half lengthways. Scoop out the seeds from one half and place it cut side down. Using a knife held at an angle, thinly slice the cucumber, cutting almost through so the slices remain attached at the base. Fan the slices out. Turn in alternate slices to form loops, then bend into a semi-circle with the loops on the outside, so that they resemble petals.

1 Using a small pair of scissors or a slim-bladed knife, slit a fresh red chilli carefully lengthways from the tip to within 1cm/$\frac{1}{2}$in of the stem end. Repeat this at regular intervals around the chilli, keeping the stem end intact, until it resembles a tassel. Slit more chillies in the same way.

2 Rinse the chillies in cold water to wash away the seeds. Place in a bowl of iced water and chill for at least 4 hours. For very curly chilli flowers, leave the bowl in the refrigerator overnight.

MEAT AND POULTRY

The wok is an excellent cooking vessel for many meat dishes, as its fast cooking ability retains the flavour and moistness of the meat. Poultry's mild taste also makes it a good protein to mix with robust oriental spices and flavours. This chapter includes a wide choice of fast and simple stir-fries such as Cashew Chicken and Spicy Shredded Beef. It also contains some delicious slow cooked, rich curries, such as Chinese Braised Pork and Yellow Chicken Curry, with depths of flavour coming from ingredients such as garlic, shallots, ginger and lemon grass.

CHICKEN AND LEMON GRASS CURRY

QUICK-COOK CURRIES, SUCH AS THIS THAI SPECIALITY, WORK WELL IN A WOK, ESPECIALLY IF YOU USE AN ELECTRIC APPLIANCE, WHICH ALLOWS YOU TO ADJUST THE HEAT FOR SUCCESSFUL SIMMERING.

SERVES FOUR

INGREDIENTS
   45ml/3 tbsp vegetable oil
   2 garlic cloves, crushed
   500g/1¼lb skinless, chicken thighs,
      boned and chopped into small
      pieces
   45ml/3 tbsp Thai fish sauce
   120ml/4fl oz/½ cup
      chicken stock
   5ml/1 tsp granulated sugar
   1 lemon grass stalk, chopped into
      4 sticks and lightly crushed
   5 kaffir lime leaves, rolled into
      cylinders and thinly sliced across,
      plus extra to garnish
   chopped roasted peanuts
      and chopped fresh coriander
      (cilantro), to garnish
For the curry paste
   1 lemon grass stalk,
      coarsely chopped
   2.5cm/1in piece fresh galangal,
      peeled and coarsely chopped
   2 kaffir lime leaves, chopped
   3 shallots, coarsely chopped
   6 coriander (cilantro) roots,
      coarsely chopped
   2 garlic cloves
   2 fresh green chillies, seeded and
      coarsely chopped
   5ml/1 tsp shrimp paste
   5ml/1 tsp ground turmeric

1 Make the curry paste. Place all the ingredients in a large mortar, or food processor, and pound with the pestle or process to a smooth paste.

2 Heat the vegetable oil in a wok or large, heavy frying pan, add the garlic and cook over a low heat, stirring frequently, until golden brown. Be careful not to let the garlic burn or it will taste bitter. Add the curry paste and stir-fry with the garlic for about 30 seconds more.

3 Add the chicken pieces to the pan and stir until thoroughly coated with the curry paste. Stir in the Thai fish sauce and chicken stock, with the sugar, and cook, stirring constantly, for 2 minutes more.

4 Add the lemon grass and lime leaves, reduce the heat and simmer for 10 minutes. If the mixture begins to dry out, add a little more stock or water.

5 Remove the lemon grass, if you like. Spoon the curry into four dishes, garnish with the lime leaves, peanuts and coriander and serve immediately.

Energy 229Kcal/959kJ; Protein 31.3g; Carbohydrate 4.3g, of which sugars 3.4g; Fat 9.7g, of which saturates 1.4g; Cholesterol 94mg; Calcium 32mg; Fibre 0.5g; Sodium 397mg.

YELLOW CHICKEN CURRY

THE PAIRING OF SLIGHTLY SWEET COCONUT MILK AND FRUIT WITH SAVOURY CHICKEN AND SPICES IS AT ONCE A COMFORTING, REFRESHING AND EXOTIC COMBINATION.

SERVES FOUR

INGREDIENTS
- 300ml/½ pint/1¼ cups chicken stock
- 30ml/2 tbsp tamarind paste mixed with a little warm water
- 15ml/1 tbsp granulated sugar
- 200ml/7fl oz/scant 1 cup coconut milk
- 1 green papaya, peeled, seeded and thinly sliced
- 250g/9oz skinless chicken breast fillets, diced
- juice of 1 lime
- lime slices, to garnish

For the curry paste
- 1 fresh red chilli, seeded and coarsely chopped
- 4 garlic cloves, coarsely chopped
- 3 shallots, coarsely chopped
- 2 lemon grass stalks, sliced
- 5cm/2in piece fresh turmeric, coarsely chopped, or 5ml/1 tsp ground turmeric
- 5ml/1 tsp shrimp paste
- 5ml/1 tsp salt

2 Pour the stock into a wok or medium pan and bring it to the boil. Stir in the curry paste. Bring back to the boil and add the tamarind juice, sugar and coconut milk. Add the papaya and chicken and cook over a medium to high heat for about 15 minutes, stirring frequently, until the chicken is cooked.

3 Stir in the lime juice, transfer to a warm dish and serve immediately, garnished with lime slices.

1 Make the yellow curry paste. Put the red chilli, garlic, shallots, lemon grass and turmeric in a mortar or food processor. Add the shrimp paste and salt. Pound or process to a paste, adding a little water if necessary.

COOK'S TIP
Fresh turmeric resembles root ginger in appearance and is a member of the same family. When preparing it, wear gloves to protect your hands from staining.

Energy 149Kcal/633kJ; Protein 17.2g; Carbohydrate 18.9g, of which sugars 17.2g; Fat 1.1g, of which saturates 0.3g; Cholesterol 50mg; Calcium 70mg; Fibre 2.8g; Sodium 153mg.

STIR-FRIED CHICKEN WITH BASIL AND CHILLI

This quick and easy chicken dish from Thailand owes its spicy flavour to fresh chillies and its pungency to Thai basil, which has a lovely aroma with hints of liquorice.

2 Add the pieces of chicken to the wok or pan, in batches if necessary, and stir-fry until the chicken changes colour.

3 Stir in the fish sauce, soy sauce and sugar. Continue to stir-fry the mixture for 3–4 minutes, or until the chicken is fully cooked and golden brown.

4 Stir in the fresh Thai basil leaves. Spoon the mixture on to a warm platter, or into individual dishes. Garnish with the chopped chillies and deep-fried Thai basil and serve immediately.

SERVES FOUR TO SIX

INGREDIENTS
  45ml/3 tbsp vegetable oil
  4 garlic cloves, thinly sliced
  2–4 fresh red chillies, seeded and
    finely chopped
  450g/1lb skinless chicken breast
    fillets, cut into bitesize pieces
  45ml/3 tbsp Thai fish sauce
  10ml/2 tsp dark soy sauce
  5ml/1 tsp granulated sugar
  10–12 fresh Thai basil leaves
  2 fresh red chillies, seeded and
    finely chopped, and about 20 deep-
    fried Thai basil leaves, to garnish

1 Heat the oil in a wok or large, heavy frying pan. Add the garlic and chillies and stir-fry over a medium heat for 1–2 minutes until the garlic is golden. Take care not to let the garlic burn, otherwise it will taste bitter.

COOK'S TIP
To deep-fry Thai basil leaves, first make sure that the leaves are completely dry or they will splutter when added to the oil. Heat vegetable or groundnut (peanut) oil in a wok or deep-fryer to 190°C/375°F or until a cube of bread, added to the oil, browns in about 40 seconds. Add the leaves and deep-fry them briefly until they are crisp and translucent – this will take only about 30–40 seconds, so watch them carefully. Lift out the leaves using a slotted spoon or wire basket and leave them to drain on kitchen paper before using.

Energy 138Kcal/576kJ; Protein 18.3g; Carbohydrate 1.9g, of which sugars 1.8g; Fat 6.4g, of which saturates 0.9g; Cholesterol 53mg; Calcium 6mg; Fibre 0.1g; Sodium 579mg.

SOUTHERN THAI CHICKEN CURRY

THIS IS A MILD COCONUT CURRY FLAVOURED WITH TURMERIC, CORIANDER AND CUMIN SEEDS, WHICH COMBINES THE CULINARY INFLUENCES OF MALAYSIA AND NEIGHBOURING THAILAND.

SERVES FOUR

INGREDIENTS
  60ml/4 tbsp vegetable oil
  1 large garlic clove, crushed
  1 chicken, weighing about 1.5kg/
    3–3½lb, chopped into
    12 large pieces
  400ml/14fl oz/1⅔ cups
    coconut cream
  250ml/8fl oz/1 cup chicken stock
  30ml/2 tbsp Thai fish sauce
  30ml/2 tbsp sugar
  juice of 2 limes
To garnish
  2 small fresh red chillies, seeded and
    finely chopped
  1 bunch spring onions (scallions),
    thinly sliced
For the curry paste
  5ml/1 tsp dried chilli flakes
  2.5ml/½ tsp salt
  5cm/2in piece fresh turmeric or
    5ml/1 tsp ground turmeric
  2.5ml/½ tsp coriander seeds
  2.5ml/½ tsp cumin seeds
  5ml/1 tsp shrimp paste

1 First make the curry paste. Put all the ingredients in a mortar, food processor or spice grinder and pound, process or grind to a smooth paste.

2 Heat the oil in a wok or frying pan and cook the garlic until golden. Add the chicken and cook until golden. Remove the chicken and set aside.

3 Reheat the oil and add the curry paste and then half the coconut cream. Cook for a few minutes until fragrant.

4 Return the chicken to the wok or pan, add the stock, mixing well, then add the remaining coconut cream, the fish sauce, sugar and lime juice. Stir well and bring to the boil, then lower the heat and simmer for 15 minutes.

5 Turn the curry into four warm serving bowls and sprinkle with the chopped fresh chillies and spring onions to garnish. Serve immediately.

COOK'S TIP
Shrimp paste has a very powerful flavour and should always be cooked before eating. Its strong, salty flavour mellows when cooked, but it still has a powerful kick, and should be used with care. Store, well wrapped, in the fridge.

Energy 686Kcal/2849kJ; Protein 46.8g; Carbohydrate 12.8g, of which sugars 12.8g; Fat 50g, of which saturates 12.8g; Cholesterol 246mg; Calcium 67mg; Fibre 0g; Sodium 352mg.

CASHEW CHICKEN

ONE OF THE MOST POPULAR ITEMS ON ANY CHINESE RESTAURANT MENU, CASHEW CHICKEN IS EASY TO RECREATE AT HOME. IT IS IMPORTANT TO HAVE THE WOK VERY HOT BEFORE ADDING THE CHICKEN OR IT WILL STEW RATHER THAN STIR-FRY. A CARBON STEEL WOK WILL GIVE GOOD RESULTS.

SERVES FOUR TO SIX

INGREDIENTS
  450g/1lb skinless chicken breast
    fillets
  1 red (bell) pepper
  2 garlic cloves
  4 dried red chillies
  30ml/2 tbsp vegetable oil
  30ml/2 tbsp oyster sauce
  15ml/1 tbsp soy sauce
  pinch of granulated sugar
  1 bunch spring onions (scallions), cut
    into 5cm/2in lengths
  175g/6oz/1½ cups cashews, roasted
  coriander (cilantro) leaves,
    to garnish

1 Remove and discard the skin from the chicken breasts and trim off any excess fat. With a sharp knife, cut the chicken into bitesize pieces and set aside.

2 Halve the red pepper, scrape out the seeds and membranes and discard, then cut the flesh into 2cm/¾in dice. Peel and thinly slice the garlic and chop the dried red chillies.

3 Preheat a wok and then heat the oil. The best way to do this is to drizzle a "necklace" of oil around the inner rim of the wok, so that it drops down to coat the entire inner surface. Make sure the coating is even by swirling the wok.

4 Add the garlic and dried chillies to the wok and stir-fry over a medium heat until golden. Do not let the garlic burn, otherwise it will taste bitter.

5 Add the chicken to the wok and stir-fry until it is cooked through, then add the red pepper. If the mixture is very dry, add a little water.

6 Stir in the oyster sauce, soy sauce and sugar. Add the spring onions and cashew nuts. Stir-fry for 1–2 minutes more, until heated through. Spoon into a warm dish and serve immediately, garnished with the coriander leaves.

COOK'S TIP
Cashews are also valued for the "fruit" under which each nut grows. Although they are known as cashew apples, these so-called fruits are actually bulbous portions of the stem. They may be pink, red or yellow in colour and the crisp, sweet flesh can be eaten raw or made into a refreshing drink. Cashew apples – and undried nuts – are rarely seen outside their growing regions.

Energy 314Kcal/1307kJ; Protein 24.7g; Carbohydrate 10.2g, of which sugars 6.2g; Fat 19.6g, of which saturates 3.7g; Cholesterol 53mg; Calcium 24mg; Fibre 1.7g; Sodium 268mg.

HIJIKI SEAWEED AND CHICKEN

THE TASTE OF THE JAPANESE SEAWEED, HIJIKI, IS SOMEWHERE BETWEEN RICE AND VEGETABLE. IT MAKES A GOOD ACCOMPANIMENT TO MEAT OR TOFU PRODUCTS, ESPECIALLY WHEN IT'S STIR-FRIED IN THE WOK FIRST WITH A LITTLE OIL.

SERVES TWO

INGREDIENTS
90g/3½oz dried hijiki seaweed
150g/5oz chicken breast portion
½ small carrot, about 5cm/2in
15ml/1 tbsp vegetable oil
100ml/3fl oz/scant ½ cup instant
   dashi powder plus 1.5ml/¼ tsp
   dashi-no-moto
30ml/2 tbsp sake
30ml/2 tbsp caster (superfine) sugar
45ml/3 tbsp shoyu
a pinch of cayenne pepper

1 Soak the hijiki in cold water for about 30 minutes. When ready to cook, it is easily crushed between the fingers. Pour into a sieve and wash under running water. Drain.

2 Peel the skin from the chicken and par-boil the skin in rapidly boiling water for 1 minute, then drain. With a sharp knife, shave off all the yellow fat from the skin. Discard the clear membrane between the fat and the skin as well. Cut the skin into thin strips about 5mm/¼in wide and 2.5cm/1in long. Cut the meat into small, bitesize chunks.

3 Peel and chop the carrot into long, narrow matchsticks.

4 Heat the oil in a wok or frying pan and stir-fry the strips of chicken skin for 5 minutes, or until golden and curled up. Add the chicken meat and keep stirring until the colour changes.

5 Add the hijiki and carrot, then stir-fry for a further minute. Add the remaining ingredients. Lower the heat and toss over the heat for 5 minutes more.

6 Remove the wok from the heat and leave to stand for about 10 minutes. Serve in small individual bowls. Sprinkle with cayenne pepper.

COOK'S TIP
Chicken skin is sometimes discarded because of its high calorie content. However, in this dish the thick yellow fat is removed from the skin before cooking, thus greatly reducing the fat content. The skin curls and becomes crisp when fried, rather like pork crackling. It tastes good but can be omitted if preferred.

Energy 224Kcal/942kJ; Protein 19g; Carbohydrate 19.8g, of which sugars 19.4g; Fat 6.4g, of which saturates 1g; Cholesterol 52mg; Calcium 24mg; Fibre 0.6g; Sodium 1658mg.

SICHUAN CHICKEN WITH KUNG PO SAUCE

THIS RECIPE, WHICH HAILS FROM THE SICHUAN REGION OF WESTERN CHINA, HAS BECOME ONE OF THE CLASSIC RECIPES IN THE CHINESE REPERTOIRE. THE COMBINATION OF YELLOW SALTED BEANS AND HOISIN, SPIKED WITH CHILLI, MAKES FOR A VERY TASTY AND SPICY SAUCE.

SERVES THREE

INGREDIENTS
   2–3 skinless chicken breast fillets,
      cut into neat pieces
   1 egg white
   10ml/2 tsp cornflour
   2.5ml/1/2 tsp salt
   30ml/2 tbsp yellow salted beans
   15ml/1 tbsp hoisin sauce
   5ml/1 tsp light brown sugar
   15ml/1 tbsp rice wine or
      medium-dry sherry
   15ml/1 tbsp wine vinegar
   4 garlic cloves, crushed
   150ml/1/4 pint/2/3 cup chicken stock
   45ml/3 tbsp sunflower oil
   2–3 dried chillies, broken into
      small pieces
   115g/4oz roasted cashew nuts
   fresh coriander (cilantro), to garnish

1 Lightly whisk the egg white in a dish, whisk in the cornflour and salt, then add the chicken and stir until coated.

COOK'S TIP
Peanuts are the classic ingredient in this dish, but cashew nuts have an even better flavour and have become popular both in home cooking and in restaurants. Use roasted peanuts if you prefer.

2 In a separate bowl, mash the salted beans with a spoon. Stir in the hoisin sauce, brown sugar, rice wine or sherry, vinegar, garlic and stock.

3 Heat a wok, add the oil and then stir-fry the chicken, turning constantly, for about 2 minutes until tender. Either drain the chicken over a bowl to collect excess oil, or lift out each piece with a slotted spoon, leaving the oil in the wok.

4 Heat the reserved oil and fry the chilli pieces for 1 minute. Return the chicken to the wok and pour in the bean sauce mixture. Bring to the boil and stir in the cashew nuts. Spoon into a heated serving dish and garnish with coriander leaves.

Energy 490Kcal/2040kJ; Protein 37.7g; Carbohydrate 12.4g, of which sugars 2.6g; Fat 31.9g, of which saturates 5.6g; Cholesterol 82mg; Calcium 24mg; Fibre 1.9g; Sodium 204mg.

FRAGRANT TARRAGON CHICKEN

CHICKEN THIGHS HAVE A PARTICULARLY GOOD FLAVOUR AND STAND UP WELL TO THE ROBUST INGREDIENTS USED IN THIS DISH. FEW PEOPLE THINK OF USING A WOK FOR BRAISING, BUT IT WORKS EXTREMELY WELL, PROVIDED YOU HAVE A SUITABLE LID THAT FITS SNUGLY.

SERVES FOUR

INGREDIENTS
   3 heads of garlic, cloves separated
      but still in their skins
   2 onions, quartered
   8 chicken thighs
   90ml/6 tbsp chopped fresh
      tarragon leaves
   8 small pickled lemons,
   30–45ml/2–3 tbsp olive oil
   750ml/1¼ pints/3 cups
      dessert wine
   250ml/8fl oz/1 cup chicken stock
   sea salt and ground black pepper
   sautéed potatoes and steamed yellow
      or green beans, to serve

1 Arrange the garlic cloves and quartered onions in the base of a large wok and lay the chicken thighs over the top in a single layer. Sprinkle the tarragon over the top of the chicken, season well with salt and ground black pepper and drizzle over the olive oil.

2 Chop the pickled lemons and add to the wok. Pour the wine and stock over and bring to the boil. Cover the wok tightly, reduce the heat to low and simmer gently for 1½ hours. Remove from the heat, and leave to stand, covered, for 10 minutes. Serve with sautéed potatoes and steamed beans.

Energy 390Kcal/1630kJ; Protein 24g; Carbohydrate 21.8g, of which sugars 17.2g; Fat 8.8g, of which saturates 1.6g; Cholesterol 105mg; Calcium 86mg; Fibre 2.7g; Sodium 122mg.

Spiced Coconut Chicken with Cardamom

You need to plan ahead to make this luxurious curry, as the chicken needs to be marinated overnight in an aromatic blend of yogurt and spices. Serve with rice.

SERVES FOUR

INGREDIENTS
    1.6kg/3½lb large chicken drumsticks
    30ml/2 tbsp sunflower oil
    400ml/14fl oz/1⅔ cups coconut milk
    4–6 large green chillies, halved
    45ml/3 tbsp finely chopped
       coriander (cilantro)
    salt and ground black pepper
    natural (plain) yogurt, to drizzle
For the marinade
    15ml/1 tbsp cardamom pods
    15ml/1 tbsp grated fresh root ginger
    10ml/2 tsp crushed garlic
    105ml/7 tbsp natural (plain) yogurt
    2 fresh green chillies, seeded and
       chopped
    5ml/1 tsp ground cumin
    5ml/1 tsp ground coriander
    5ml/1 tsp ground turmeric
    finely grated rind and juice of 1 lime

1 Make the marinade. Smash the cardamom pods in a pestle so the seeds separate from the husks. Discard the husks. Put the cardamom seeds, ginger, garlic, half the yogurt, green chillies, cumin, coriander, turmeric and lime rind and juice in a blender. Process until smooth, season and pour into a large glass bowl.

2 Add the chicken to the bowl and toss to coat. Cover and marinate in the refrigerator for 6–8 hours, or overnight.

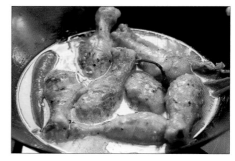

3 Heat the oil in a large, non-stick wok over a low heat. Add the chicken, reserving the marinade. Add the chicken to the wok and brown all over, then add the coconut milk, remaining yogurt, reserved marinade and green chillies and bring to the boil.

4 Reduce the heat and simmer gently, uncovered, for 30–35 minutes. Check the seasoning, adding more if needed. Stir in the coriander, ladle into warmed bowls and serve drizzled with yogurt.

Energy 691Kcal/2906kJ; Protein 107.7g; Carbohydrate 6.2g, of which sugars 6.1g; Fat 26.5g, of which saturates 6.5g; Cholesterol 540mg; Calcium 142mg; Fibre 0.6g; Sodium 805mg.

SOUTHERN CURRIED NOODLES

CHICKEN OR PORK CAN BE USED IN THIS TASTY DISH. IT IS SO QUICK AND EASY TO PREPARE AND COOKS IN NEXT TO NO TIME, MAKING IT THE PERFECT SNACK FOR BUSY PEOPLE.

SERVES TWO

INGREDIENTS
30ml/2 tbsp vegetable oil
10ml/2 tsp magic paste
1 lemon grass stalk, finely chopped
5ml/1 tsp Thai red curry paste
90g/3½ oz skinless chicken breast
   fillets or pork fillet (tenderloin),
   sliced into slivers
30ml/2 tbsp light soy sauce
400ml/14fl oz/1⅔ cups coconut milk
2 kaffir lime leaves, rolled into
   cylinders and thinly sliced
250g/9oz dried medium egg noodles
90g/3½ oz Chinese leaves (Chinese
   cabbage), shredded
90g/3½ oz spinach or watercress,
   shredded
juice of 1 lime
small bunch fresh coriander
   (cilantro), chopped

1 Heat the oil in a wok or large, heavy frying pan. Add the magic paste and lemon grass and stir-fry over a low to medium heat for 4–5 seconds, until they give off their aroma.

2 Stir in the curry paste, then add the chicken or pork. Stir-fry over a medium to high heat for 2 minutes, until the chicken or pork is coated in the paste and seared on all sides.

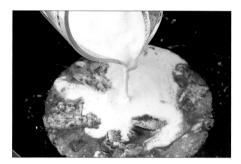

3 Add the soy sauce, coconut milk and sliced lime leaves. Bring to a simmer, then add the noodles. Simmer gently for 4 minutes, tossing the mixture occasionally to make sure that the noodles cook evenly.

4 Add the Chinese leaves and the spinach or watercress. Stir well. Add the lime juice. Spoon into a warmed bowl, sprinkle with the coriander and serve.

Energy 709Kcal/2989kJ; Protein 29.5g; Carbohydrate 102.1g, of which sugars 14.6g; Fat 23.1g, of which saturates 4.8g; Cholesterol 69mg; Calcium 251mg; Fibre 5.5g; Sodium 1666mg.

CURRIED CHICKEN AND RICE

THIS SIMPLE ONE-WOK MEAL IS PERFECT FOR CASUAL ENTERTAINING. IT CAN BE MADE USING VIRTUALLY ANY TENDER PIECES OF MEAT OR STIR-FRY VEGETABLES THAT YOU HAVE TO HAND. THE RICE IS DELICIOUSLY TASTY AFTER BEING COOKED IN THE STOCK.

SERVES FOUR

INGREDIENTS
   60ml/4 tbsp vegetable oil
   4 garlic cloves, finely chopped
   1 chicken (about 1.5kg/3–3½lb)
      or chicken pieces, skinned and
      boned and cut into bitesize pieces
   5ml/1 tsp garam masala
   450g/1lb/2⅔ cups jasmine rice,
      rinsed and drained
   10ml/2 tsp salt
   1 litre/1¾ pints/4 cups
      chicken stock
   small bunch fresh coriander
      (cilantro), chopped, to garnish

COOK'S TIP
You will probably need to brown the chicken in batches, so don't be tempted to add too much chicken at once.

1 Heat the oil in a wok or flameproof casserole, which has a lid. Add the garlic and cook over a low to medium heat until golden brown. Add the chicken, increase the heat and brown the pieces on all sides (see Cook's Tip).

2 Add the garam masala, stir well to coat the chicken all over in the spice, then tip in the drained rice. Add the salt and stir to mix.

3 Pour in the stock, stir well, then cover the wok or casserole and bring to the boil. Reduce the heat to low and simmer gently for 10 minutes, until the rice is cooked and tender.

4 Lift the wok or casserole off the heat, leaving the lid on, and leave for 10 minutes. Fluff up the rice grains with a fork and spoon on to a platter. Sprinkle with the coriander and serve immediately.

Energy 715Kcal/2994kJ; Protein 56.3g; Carbohydrate 89.8g, of which sugars 0g; Fat 13.8g, of which saturates 1.9g; Cholesterol 140mg; Calcium 32mg; Fibre 0g; Sodium 1103mg.

JUNGLE CURRY OF GUINEA FOWL

A TRADITIONAL WILD FOOD COUNTRY CURRY FROM THE NORTH-CENTRAL REGION OF THAILAND, THIS DISH CAN BE MADE USING ANY GAME, FISH OR CHICKEN. GUINEA FOWL IS NOT TYPICAL OF THAI CUISINE, BUT IS A POPULAR AND WIDELY AVAILABLE GAME BIRD IN THE WEST.

SERVES FOUR

INGREDIENTS

1 guinea fowl or similar game bird
15ml/1 tbsp vegetable oil
10ml/2 tsp Thai green curry paste
15ml/1 tbsp Thai fish sauce
2.5cm/1in piece fresh galangal,
    peeled and finely chopped
15ml/1 tbsp fresh green peppercorns
3 kaffir lime leaves, torn
15ml/1 tbsp whisky,
    preferably Mekhong
300ml/½ pint/1¼ cups
    chicken stock
50g/2oz snake beans or yard-long
    beans, cut into 2.5cm/1in lengths
    (about ½ cup)
225g/8oz/3¼ cups chestnut
    mushrooms, sliced
1 piece drained canned bamboo
    shoot, about 50g/2oz, shredded
5ml/1 tsp dried chilli flakes, to
    garnish (optional)

1 Cut up the guinea fowl, remove and discard the skin, then take all the meat off the bones. Chop the meat into bitesize pieces and set aside.

2 Heat the oil in a wok or frying pan and add the curry paste. Stir-fry over a medium heat for 30 seconds, until the paste gives off its aroma.

3 Add the fish sauce and the guinea fowl meat and stir-fry until the meat is browned all over. Add the galangal, peppercorns, lime leaves and whisky, then pour in the stock.

4 Bring to the boil. Add the vegetables, return to a simmer and cook gently for 2–3 minutes, until they are just cooked. Spoon into a dish, sprinkle with chilli flakes, if you like, and serve.

COOK'S TIPS
• Guinea fowl originated in West Africa and was regarded as a game bird. However, it has been domesticated in Europe for over 500 years. They range in size from 675g/1½lb to 2kg/4½lb, but about 1.2kg/2½lb is average. American readers could substitute two or three Cornish hens, depending on size.
• Fresh green peppercorns are simply unripe berries. They are sold on the stem and look rather like miniature Brussels sprout stalks. Look for them at Thai supermarkets. If unavailable, substitute bottled green peppercorns, but rinse well and drain them first.

Energy 321Kcal/1345kJ; Protein 42.2g; Carbohydrate 1.1g, of which sugars 0.7g; Fat 15g, of which saturates 4.4g; Cholesterol 0mg; Calcium 73mg; Fibre 1.1g; Sodium 127mg.

CHINESE DUCK CURRY

THIS RICHLY SPICED CURRY ILLUSTRATES HOW HARMONIOUSLY FIVE-SPICE POWDER MARRIES THE FLAVOURS OF DUCK, GINGER AND BUTTERNUT SQUASH. THE DUCK IS BEST MARINATED FOR AS LONG AS POSSIBLE, ALTHOUGH IT TASTES GOOD EVEN IF YOU ONLY HAVE TIME TO MARINATE IT BRIEFLY.

SERVES FOUR

INGREDIENTS

    4 duck breast portions, skinned
    30ml/2 tbsp five-spice powder
    30ml/2 tbsp sesame oil
    grated rind and juice of 1 orange
    1 medium butternut squash, peeled
      and cubed
    10ml/2 tsp Thai red curry paste
    30ml/2 tbsp Thai fish sauce
    15ml/1 tbsp palm sugar (jaggery) or
      light muscovado (brown) sugar
    300ml/½ pint/1¼ cups coconut milk
    2 fresh red chillies, seeded
    4 kaffir lime leaves, torn
    small bunch coriander (cilantro),
      chopped, to garnish

1 Cut the duck meat into bitesize pieces and place in a bowl with the five-spice powder, sesame oil and orange rind and juice. Stir well to mix all the ingredients and coat the duck in the marinade. Cover the bowl with clear film (plastic wrap) and set aside in a cool place to marinate for at least 15 minutes.

2 Meanwhile, bring a pan of water to the boil. Add the squash and cook for 10–15 minutes, until just tender. Drain well and set aside.

3 Pour the marinade from the duck into a wok and heat until boiling. Stir in the curry paste and cook for 2–3 minutes, until well blended and fragrant. Add the duck and cook for 3–4 minutes, stirring constantly, until browned on all sides.

4 Add the fish sauce and palm sugar and cook for 2 minutes more. Stir in the coconut milk until the mixture is smooth, then add the cooked squash, with the chillies and lime leaves.

5 Simmer gently, stirring frequently, for 5 minutes, then spoon into a dish, sprinkle with the coriander and serve with noodles.

Energy 295Kcal/1241kJ; Protein 31.4g; Carbohydrate 13.3g, of which sugars 12.3g; Fat 15.9g, of which saturates 3.1g; Cholesterol 165mg; Calcium 102mg; Fibre 2g; Sodium 427mg.

RED DUCK CURRY WITH PEA AUBERGINES

THIS TASTY CURRY NEEDS TO BE SIMMERED AND THEN LEFT TO STAND TO ALLOW THE FLAVOURS TO BLEND BEAUTIFULLY. USE AN ELECTRIC WOK IF YOU HAVE ONE TO MAINTAIN THE STEADY TEMPERATURE NEEDED FOR GENTLE SIMMERING.

SERVES FOUR

INGREDIENTS
- 4 duck breast portions
- 400ml/14fl oz can coconut milk
- 200ml/7fl oz/scant 1 cup chicken stock
- 30ml/2 tbsp red Thai curry paste
- 8 spring onions (scallions), finely sliced
- 10ml/2 tsp grated fresh root ginger
- 30ml/2 tbsp Chinese rice wine
- 15ml/1 tbsp fish sauce
- 15ml/1 tbsp soy sauce
- 2 lemon grass stalks, halved lengthways
- 3–4 kaffir lime leaves
- 300g/11oz pea aubergines (eggplants)
- 10ml/2 tsp sugar
- salt and ground black pepper
- 10–12 fresh basil and mint leaves, to garnish
- steamed jasmine rice, to serve

4 Remove the wok from the heat and leave to stand, covered, for about 15 minutes. Season to taste

5 Serve the duck curry ladled into shallow bowls, garnished with fresh mint and basil leaves. Serve with steamed jasmine rice.

COOK'S TIP
Tiny pea aubergines (eggplants) are sold in Asian stores. If you can't find them, use regular aubergines cut into chunks.

1 Using a sharp knife, cut the duck breast portions into neat bitesize pieces.

2 Place a wok over a low heat and add the coconut milk, stock, curry paste, spring onions, ginger, rice wine, fish and soy sauces, lemon grass and lime leaves. Stir well to mix, then bring to the boil over a medium heat.

3 Add the duck, aubergines and sugar to the wok and gently simmer for 25–30 minutes, stirring occasionally.

Energy 241Kcal/1017kJ; Protein 31.1g; Carbohydrate 10.2g, of which sugars 10g; Fat 10.5g, of which saturates 2.3g; Cholesterol 165mg; Calcium 65mg; Fibre 1.8g; Sodium 546mg.

GREEN BEEF CURRY <u>WITH</u> THAI AUBERGINES

This is a very quick curry so be sure to use good quality meat. Sirloin is recommended, but tender rump steak could be used instead. If you buy the curry paste, there's very little additional preparation, but you could make it from scratch if you prefer.

SERVES FOUR TO SIX

INGREDIENTS

- 450g/1lb sirloin steak
- 15ml/1 tbsp vegetable oil
- 45ml/3 tbsp Thai green curry paste
- 600ml/1 pint/2½ cups coconut milk
- 4 kaffir lime leaves, torn
- 15–30ml/1–2 tbsp Thai fish sauce
- 5ml/1 tsp palm sugar (jaggery) or light muscovado (brown) sugar
- 150g/5oz small Thai aubergines (eggplant), halved
- small handful of fresh Thai basil
- 2 fresh green chillies, to garnish

1 Trim off any excess fat from the beef. Using a sharp knife, cut it into long, thin strips. This is easiest to do if it is well chilled. Set it aside.

2 Heat the oil in a wok. Add the curry paste and cook for 1–2 minutes, until it you can smell the fragrances.

3 Stir in half the coconut milk, a little at a time. Cook, stirring frequently, for about 5–6 minutes, until an oily sheen appears on the surface of the liquid.

4 Add the beef to the pan with the kaffir lime leaves, Thai fish sauce, sugar and aubergine halves. Cook for 2–3 minutes, then stir in the remaining coconut milk.

5 Bring back to a simmer and cook until the meat and aubergines are tender. Stir in the Thai basil just before serving. Finely shred the green chillies and use to garnish the curry.

GREEN CURRY PASTE
To make the curry paste from scratch, put 15 fresh green chillies, 2 chopped lemon grass stalks, 3 sliced shallots, 2 garlic cloves, 15ml/1 tbsp chopped galangal, 4 chopped kaffir lime leaves, 2.5ml/½ tsp grated kaffir lime rind, 5ml/1 tsp chopped coriander root, 6 black peppercorns, 5ml/1 tsp each roasted coriander and cumin seeds, 15ml/1 tbsp granulated sugar, 5ml/1 tsp salt and 5ml/1 tsp shrimp paste into a food processor and process until smooth. Gradually add 30ml/2 tbsp vegetable oil, processing after each addition.

Energy 146Kcal/615kJ; Protein 18.2g; Carbohydrate 6.2g, of which sugars 6.1g; Fat 5.6g, of which saturates 1.9g; Cholesterol 38mg; Calcium 36mg; Fibre 0.5g; Sodium 163mg.

DRY BEEF CURRY <u>WITH</u> PEANUT <u>AND</u> LIME

ALTHOUGH THIS IS CALLED A DRY CURRY, THE DESCRIPTION SIMPLY MEANS THE MEAT ISN'T SWIMMING IN LIQUID. THE METHOD OF COOKING IN THE WOK ENSURES THAT THE BEEF ABSORBS THE COCONUT MILK AND PEANUT BUTTER MIXTURE AND STAYS SUCCULENT.

SERVES FOUR TO SIX

INGREDIENTS
    400g/14oz can coconut milk
    900g/2lb stewing steak,
      finely chopped
    300ml/½ pint/1¼ cups beef stock
    30ml/2 tbsp crunchy peanut butter
    juice of 2 limes
    lime slices, shredded coriander
      (cilantro) and fresh red chilli slices,
      to garnish
For the red curry paste
    30ml/2 tbsp coriander seeds
    5ml/1 tsp cumin seeds
    seeds from 6 green cardamom pods
    2.5ml/½ tsp grated or ground nutmeg
    1.5ml/¼ tsp ground cloves
    2.5ml/½ tsp ground cinnamon
    20ml/4 tsp paprika
    pared rind of 1 mandarin orange,
      finely chopped
    4–5 small fresh red chillies, seeded
      and finely chopped
    25ml/1½ tsp granulated sugar
    2.5ml/½ tsp salt
    1 piece lemon grass, about 10cm/4in
      long, shredded
    3 garlic cloves, crushed
    2cm/¾in piece fresh galangal,
      peeled and finely chopped
    4 red shallots, finely chopped
    1 piece shrimp paste,
      2cm/¾in square
    50g/2oz coriander (cilantro) root or
      stem, chopped
    juice of ½ lime
    30ml/2 tbsp vegetable oil

1 Strain the coconut milk into a bowl, retaining the thicker coconut milk in the strainer or sieve.

2 Pour the thin coconut milk from the bowl into a large, heavy pan, then scrape in half the residue from the sieve. Reserve the remaining thick coconut milk. Add the chopped steak. Pour in the beef stock and bring to the boil. Reduce the heat, cover the pan and simmer gently for 50 minutes.

3 Make the curry paste. Dry-fry all the seeds for 1–2 minutes. Tip into a bowl and add the nutmeg, cloves, cinnamon, paprika and orange rind. Pound the chillies with the sugar and salt. Add the spice mixture, lemon grass, garlic, galangal, shallots and shrimp paste and pound to a paste. Work in the coriander, lime juice and oil.

4 Strain the beef, reserving the cooking liquid, and place a cupful of liquid in a wok. Stir in 30–45ml/2–3 tbsp of the curry paste, according to taste. Boil rapidly until all the liquid has evaporated. Stir in the reserved thick coconut milk, the peanut butter and the beef. Simmer, uncovered, for 15–20 minutes, adding a little more cooking liquid if the mixture starts to stick to the pan, but keep the curry dry.

5 Just before serving, stir in the lime juice. Serve in warmed bowls, garnished with the lime slices, shredded coriander and sliced red chillies.

VARIATION
The curry is equally delicious made with lean leg or shoulder of lamb.

Energy 296Kcal/1238kJ; Protein 35.2g; Carbohydrate 4.9g, of which sugars 4.5g; Fat 15.2g, of which saturates 4.8g; Cholesterol 103mg; Calcium 66mg; Fibre 0.7g; Sodium 262mg.

STIR-FRIED BEEF <u>IN</u> OYSTER SAUCE

THIS IS ANOTHER SIMPLE BUT DELICIOUS RECIPE. IT IS OFTEN MADE WITH JUST ONE TYPE OF MUSHROOM, SUCH AS OYSTER, BUT USING A MIXTURE MAKES THE DISH MORE INTERESTING. OYSTER SAUCE ADDS A SAVOURY DEPTH TO THE DISH AND IS AN ESSENTIAL INGREDIENT.

3 Heat half the oil in a wok or large, heavy frying pan. Add the garlic and ginger and cook for 1–2 minutes, until fragrant. Drain the steak, add it to the wok or pan and stir well to separate the strips. Cook, stirring frequently, for a further 1–2 minutes, until the steak is browned all over and tender. Remove from the wok or pan and set aside.

4 Heat the remaining oil in the wok or pan. Add the shiitake, oyster and straw mushrooms. Stir-fry over a medium heat until golden brown.

5 Return the steak to the wok and mix it with the mushrooms. Spoon in the oyster sauce and sugar, mix well, then add ground black pepper to taste. Toss over the heat until all the ingredients are thoroughly combined.

6 Stir in the spring onions. Tip the mixture on to a serving platter, garnish with the strips of red chilli and serve.

SERVES FOUR TO SIX

INGREDIENTS
    450g/1lb rump (round) or sirloin
      steak
    30ml/2 tbsp soy sauce
    15ml/1 tbsp cornflour (cornstarch)
    45ml/3 tbsp groundnut (peanut) oil
      or vegetable oil for stir-frying
    15ml/1 tbsp chopped garlic
    15ml/1 tbsp chopped fresh
      root ginger
    225g/8oz/3¼ cups mixed mushrooms
      such as shiitake, oyster and straw
    30ml/2 tbsp oyster sauce
    5ml/1 tsp granulated sugar
    4 spring onions (scallions), cut into
      short lengths
    ground black pepper
    2 fresh red chillies, seeded and cut
      into strips, to garnish

1 Place the steak in the freezer for 30–40 minutes, until firm, then, using a sharp knife, slice it on the diagonal into long thin strips.

2 Mix together the soy sauce and cornflour in a large bowl. Add the steak, turning to coat well, cover with clear film (plastic wrap) and leave to marinate at room temperature for 1–2 hours.

Energy 160Kcal/670kJ; Protein 17.6g; Carbohydrate 2.9g, of which sugars 2.7g; Fat 8.8g, of which saturates 2g; Cholesterol 44mg; Calcium 10mg; Fibre 0.6g; Sodium 485mg.

THAI CRISPY NOODLES WITH BEEF

WHEN IT COMES TO VALUE FOR MONEY, RICE VERMICELLI IS SOMETHING SPECIAL — WHEN IT IS ADDED TO THE HOT OIL IT EXPANDS TO AT LEAST FOUR TIMES ITS ORIGINAL SIZE. THE STRANDS ALSO BECOME CRISP AND CRUNCHY, ADDING A GREAT CONTRAST TO THE BEEF AND VEGETABLE STIR-FRY.

SERVES FOUR

INGREDIENTS
  450g/1lb rump (round) steak
  teriyaki sauce, for brushing
  175g/6oz rice vermicelli
  groundnut (peanut) oil, for deep-
    frying and stir-frying
  8 spring onions (scallions),
    diagonally sliced
  2 garlic cloves, crushed
  4–5 carrots, cut into julienne strips
  1–2 fresh red chillies, seeded and
    finely sliced
  2 small courgettes (zucchini),
    diagonally sliced
  5ml/1 tsp grated fresh root ginger
  60ml/4 tbsp rice vinegar
  90ml/6 tbsp light soy sauce
  about 475ml/16fl oz/2 cups
    beef stock

1 Beat the steak to about 2.5cm/1in thick. Place in a shallow dish, brush generously with the teriyaki sauce and set aside for 2–4 hours to marinate.

2 Separate the rice vermicelli into manageable loops. Pour oil into a large wok to a depth of about 5cm/2in, and heat until a strand of vermicelli cooks as soon as it is lowered into the oil.

3 Carefully add a loop of vermicelli to the oil. Almost immediately, turn to cook on the other side, then remove and drain on kitchen paper. Repeat with the remaining loops. Transfer the cooked noodles to a deep serving bowl and keep them warm.

4 Strain the oil from the wok into a heatproof bowl and set it aside. Return 15ml/1 tbsp oil to a clean wok. When it sizzles, fry the steak for about 30 seconds on each side, until browned. Transfer to a board and cut into thick slices. The meat should be well browned on the outside but still pink inside. Set aside.

5 Add a little extra oil to the wok, add the spring onions, garlic and carrots and stir-fry over a medium heat for 5–6 minutes, until the carrots are slightly soft and have a glazed appearance. Add the chillies, courgettes and ginger and stir-fry for 1–2 minutes.

6 Stir in the rice vinegar, soy sauce and stock. Cook for 4 minutes, or until the sauce has thickened slightly. Return the slices of steak to the wok and cook for a further 1–2 minutes.

7 Spoon the steak, vegetables and sauce over the noodles and toss lightly and carefully to mix. Serve immediately.

COOK'S TIP
As soon as you add the meat mixture to the noodles, they will begin to soften in the sauce. If you wish to keep a few crispy noodles, leave some on the surface so that they do not come into contact with the hot liquid.

Energy 410Kcal/1712kJ; Protein 30.7g; Carbohydrate 41.4g, of which sugars 6.6g; Fat 13.5g, of which saturates 3g; Cholesterol 66mg; Calcium 49mg; Fibre 1.9g; Sodium 1687mg.

BEEF AND BUTTERNUT SQUASH WITH CHILLI

Stir-fried beef and sweet, orange-fleshed squash flavoured with warm spices, oyster sauce and fresh herbs makes a robust main course when served with rice or egg noodles. The addition of chilli and fresh root ginger gives the dish a wonderful vigorous bite.

SERVES FOUR

INGREDIENTS

   30ml/2 tbsp sunflower oil
   2 onions, cut into thick slices
   500g/1¼lb butternut squash,
      peeled, seeded and cut into thin
      strips
   675g/1½lb fillet steak
      (beef tenderloin)
   60ml/4 tbsp soy sauce
   90g/3½oz/½ cup golden caster
      (superfine) sugar
   1 fresh bird's eye chilli, seeded
      and chopped
   15ml/1 tbsp finely shredded fresh
      root ginger
   30ml/2 tbsp Thai fish sauce
   5ml/1 tsp ground star anise
   5ml/1 tsp five-spice powder
   15ml/1 tbsp oyster sauce
   4 spring onions (scallions), shredded
   a small handful of sweet basil leaves
   a small handful of mint leaves

1 Heat a wok over a medium-high heat and add the oil, trickling it down just below the rim so that it coats the surface. When hot, stir in the onions and squash. Stir-fry for 2–3 minutes, then reduce the heat, cover and cook gently for 5–6 minutes, or until the vegetables are just tender.

2 Place the beef between 2 sheets of clear film (plastic wrap) and beat, with a mallet or rolling pin, until thin. Using a sharp knife, cut into thin strips.

3 In a separate wok, mix the soy sauce, sugar, chilli, ginger, fish sauce, star anise, five-spice powder and oyster sauce. Stir-fry for 3–4 minutes.

4 Add the beef to the soy sauce mixture in the wok and cook over a high heat for 3–4 minutes. Remove from the heat. Add the onion and squash slices to the beef and toss well with the spring onions and herbs. Serve immediately.

Energy 500Kcal/2093kJ; Protein 41.3g; Carbohydrate 36.9g, of which sugars 33.8g; Fat 21.7g, of which saturates 7.2g; Cholesterol 98mg; Calcium 91mg; Fibre 2.9g; Sodium 1243mg.

SPICY SHREDDED BEEF

THE ESSENCE OF THIS RECIPE IS THAT THE BEEF IS CUT INTO VERY FINE STRIPS BEFORE BEING STIR-FRIED. THIS IS EASIER TO ACHIEVE IF THE PIECE OF BEEF IS PLACED IN THE FREEZER FOR 30 MINUTES UNTIL IT IS VERY FIRM BEFORE BEING SLICED WITH A SHARP KNIFE.

SERVES TWO

INGREDIENTS

225g/8oz rump (round) steak
15ml/1 tbsp each light and dark
   soy sauce
15ml/1 tbsp rice wine or
   medium-dry sherry
5ml/1 tsp dark brown soft sugar or
   golden granulated sugar
90ml/6 tbsp vegetable oil
1 large onion, thinly sliced
2.5cm/1in piece fresh root ginger,
   peeled and grated
1–2 carrots, cut into matchsticks
2–3 fresh or dried chillies, halved,
   seeded (optional) and chopped
salt and ground black pepper
fresh chives, to garnish

3 Heat a wok and add half the oil. When it is hot, stir-fry the onion and ginger for 3–4 minutes, then transfer to a plate. Add the carrot, stir-fry for 3–4 minutes until slightly softened, then transfer to a plate and keep warm.

4 Heat the remaining oil in the wok, then quickly add the beef, with the marinade, followed by the chillies.

5 Cook over high heat for 2 minutes, stirring all the time. Return the fried onion and ginger to the wok and stir-fry for 1 minute more.

6 Season with salt and pepper to taste, cover and cook for 30 seconds. Spoon the meat into two warmed bowls and add the strips of carrots. Garnish with fresh chives and serve.

1 With a sharp knife, slice the well-chilled beef very thinly, then cut each slice into fine strips or shreds.

2 Mix together the light and dark soy sauces with the rice wine or sherry and sugar in a bowl. Add the strips of beef and stir well to ensure they are evenly coated with the marinade.

COOK'S TIP
Remove and discard the seeds from the chillies before you chop them – unless, of course, you like really fiery food. In which case, you could add some or all of the seeds with the chopped chillies.

Energy 532Kcal/2207kJ; Protein 27.3g; Carbohydrate 19.3g, of which sugars 15.4g; Fat 38.1g, of which saturates 5.8g; Cholesterol 66mg; Calcium 59mg; Fibre 3.3g; Sodium 1154mg.

FRIED RICE WITH BEEF

ONE OF THE JOYS OF WOK COOKING IS THE EASE AND SPEED WITH WHICH A REALLY GOOD MEAL CAN BE PREPARED. THIS DELECTABLE BEEF AND RICE STIR-FRY CAN BE ON THE TABLE IN 15 MINUTES.

SERVES FOUR

INGREDIENTS

    200g/7oz beef steak, chilled
    15ml/1 tbsp vegetable oil
    2 garlic cloves,
      finely chopped
    1 egg
    250g/9oz/2¼ cups cooked
      jasmine rice
    ½ medium head broccoli,
      coarsely chopped
    30ml/2 tbsp dark soy sauce
    15ml/1 tbsp light soy sauce
    5ml/1 tsp palm sugar (jaggery) or
      light muscovado (brown) sugar
    15ml/1 tbsp Thai fish sauce
    ground black pepper
    chilli sauce, to serve

1 Trim the steak and cut into very thin strips with a sharp knife.

2 Heat the oil in a wok or frying pan and cook the garlic over a low to medium heat until golden. Do not let it burn. Increase the heat to high, add the steak and stir-fry for 2 minutes.

3 Move the pieces of beef to the edges of the wok or pan and break the egg into the centre. When the egg starts to set, stir-fry it with the meat.

4 Add the rice and toss all the contents of the wok together, scraping up any residue on the base, then add the broccoli, soy sauces, sugar and fish sauce and stir-fry for 2 minutes more. Season to taste with pepper and serve immediately with chilli sauce.

COOK'S TIP

Soy sauce is made from fermented soya beans. The first extraction is sold as light soy sauce and has a delicate, "beany" fragrance. Dark soy sauce has been allowed to mature for longer.

Energy 385Kcal/1606kJ; Protein 20.7g; Carbohydrate 52.7g, of which sugars 2.5g; Fat 9.8g, of which saturates 2.8g; Cholesterol 81mg; Calcium 59mg; Fibre 1.6g; Sodium 590mg.

FRIED RICE WITH PORK

THIS IS GREAT FOR USING UP LAST NIGHT'S LEFTOVER RICE, BUT FOR SAFETY'S SAKE, IT MUST HAVE BEEN COOLED QUICKLY AND KEPT IN THE REFRIGERATOR, THEN FRIED UNTIL THOROUGHLY HEATED.

SERVES FOUR TO SIX

INGREDIENTS
  45ml/3 tbsp vegetable oil
  1 onion, chopped
  15ml/1 tbsp chopped garlic
  115g/4oz pork, cut into small cubes
  2 eggs, beaten
  500g/2¼lb/4 cups cooked rice
  30ml/2 tbsp Thai fish sauce
  15ml/1 tbsp dark soy sauce
  2.5ml/½ tsp caster (superfine) sugar
  4 spring onions (scallions),
    finely sliced, sliced fresh red
    chillies, and 1 lime, cut into
    wedges, to serve

COOK'S TIP
To make 1kg/2¼lb/4 cups cooked rice,
you will need approximately 400g/14oz/
2 cups uncooked rice.

1 Heat the oil in a wok or large frying pan. Add the onion and garlic and cook for about 2 minutes until softened.

2 Add the pork to the softened onion and garlic. Stir-fry until the pork changes colour and is cooked.

3 Add the eggs and cook until scrambled into small lumps.

4 Add the rice and continue to stir and toss, to coat it with the oil and prevent it from sticking.

5 Add the fish sauce, soy sauce and sugar and mix well. Continue to fry until the rice is thoroughly heated. Spoon into warmed individual bowls and serve, with sliced spring onions, chillies and lime wedges.

Energy 343Kcal/1448kJ; Protein 11.2g; Carbohydrate 54.3g, of which sugars 2.2g; Fat 10.6g, of which saturates 2g; Cholesterol 82mg; Calcium 51mg; Fibre 0.6g; Sodium 220mg.

CURRIED PORK <u>WITH</u> PICKLED GARLIC

THIS VERY RICH CURRY IS BEST ACCOMPANIED BY LOTS OF PLAIN RICE AND PERHAPS A LIGHT VEGETABLE DISH. IT COULD SERVE FOUR WITH A VEGETABLE CURRY. ASIAN STORES SELL PICKLED GARLIC. IT IS WELL WORTH INVESTING IN A JAR, AS THE TASTE IS SWEET AND DELICIOUS.

SERVES TWO

INGREDIENTS

    130g/4½oz lean pork steaks
    30ml/2 tbsp vegetable oil
    1 garlic clove, crushed
    15ml/1 tbsp Thai red curry paste
    130ml/4½fl oz/generous ½ cup
      coconut cream
    2.5cm/1in piece fresh root ginger,
      finely chopped
    30ml/2 tbsp vegetable or
      chicken stock
    30ml/2 tbsp Thai fish sauce
    5ml/1 tsp granulated sugar
    2.5ml/½ tsp ground turmeric
    10ml/2 tsp lemon juice
    4 pickled garlic cloves,
      finely chopped
    strips of lemon and lime rind,
      to garnish

1 Place the pork steaks in the freezer for 30–40 minutes, until firm, then, using a sharp knife, cut the meat into fine slivers, trimming off any excess fat.

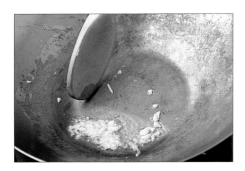

2 Heat the oil in a wok or large, heavy frying pan and cook the garlic over a low to medium heat until golden brown. Do not let it burn. Add the curry paste and stir it in well.

3 Add the coconut cream and stir until the liquid begins to reduce and thicken. Stir in the pork. Cook for 2 minutes more, until the pork is cooked through.

4 Add the ginger, stock, fish sauce, sugar and turmeric, stirring constantly, then add the lemon juice and pickled garlic and heat through. Serve in bowls, garnished with strips of rind.

Energy 227Kcal/947kJ; Protein 16.3g; Carbohydrate 9.8g, of which sugars 6.1g; Fat 14g, of which saturates 2.4g; Cholesterol 41mg; Calcium 30mg; Fibre 1g; Sodium 474mg.

SWEET AND SOUR PORK, THAI-STYLE

IT WAS THE CHINESE WHO ORIGINALLY CREATED SWEET AND SOUR COOKING, BUT THE THAIS ALSO DO IT VERY WELL. THIS VERSION HAS A FRESHER AND CLEANER FLAVOUR THAN THE ORIGINAL. IT MAKES A SUBSTANTIAL MEAL WHEN SERVED WITH RICE.

SERVES FOUR

INGREDIENTS

- 350g/12oz lean pork
- 30ml/2 tbsp vegetable oil
- 4 garlic cloves, thinly sliced
- 1 small red onion, sliced
- 30ml/2 tbsp Thai fish sauce
- 15ml/1 tbsp granulated sugar
- 1 red (bell) pepper, seeded and diced
- ½ cucumber, seeded and sliced
- 2 plum tomatoes, cut into wedges
- 115g/4oz piece of fresh pineapple, cut into small chunks
- 2 spring onions (scallions), cut into short lengths
- ground black pepper
- coriander (cilantro) leaves and spring onions (scallions), shredded to garnish

1 Place the pork in the freezer for 30–40 minutes, until firm. Using a sharp knife, cut it into thin strips.

2 Heat the oil in a wok or large frying pan. Add the garlic. Cook over a medium heat until golden, then add the pork and stir-fry for 4–5 minutes. Add the onion slices and toss to mix.

3 Add the fish sauce, sugar and ground black pepper to taste. Toss the mixture over the heat for 3–4 minutes more.

4 Stir in the red pepper, cucumber, tomatoes, pineapple and spring onions. Stir-fry for 3–4 minutes more, then spoon into a bowl. Garnish with the coriander and spring onions and serve.

Energy 211Kcal/881kJ; Protein 20.3g; Carbohydrate 11.8g, of which sugars 10.7g; Fat 9.5g, of which saturates 2g; Cholesterol 55mg; Calcium 31mg; Fibre 2g; Sodium 70mg.

STIR-FRIED PORK WITH DRIED SHRIMP

YOU MIGHT EXPECT THE DRIED SHRIMPS TO GIVE THIS DISH A FISHY FLAVOUR, BUT INSTEAD THEY SIMPLY IMPART A DELICIOUS SAVOURY TASTE, WHICH GOES VERY WELL WITH THE PORK AND WILTED GREENS. THIS IS GOOD JUST AS IT IS, BUT COULD BE SERVED WITH NOODLES OR JASMINE RICE.

SERVES FOUR

INGREDIENTS

    250g/9oz pork fillet
      (tenderloin), sliced
    30ml/2 tbsp vegetable oil
    2 garlic cloves, finely chopped
    45ml/3 tbsp dried shrimps
    10ml/2 tsp dried shrimp paste
    30ml/2 tbsp soy sauce
    juice of 1 lime
    15ml/1 tbsp palm sugar (jaggery) or
      light muscovado (brown) sugar
    1 small fresh red or green chilli,
      seeded and finely chopped
    4 pak choi (bok choy) or 450g/1lb
      spring greens (collards), shredded

1 Place the pork in the freezer for about 30 minutes, until firm. Using a sharp knife, cut it into thin slices.

2 Heat the oil in a wok or frying pan and cook the garlic until golden brown. Add the pork and stir-fry for about 4 minutes, until just cooked through.

3 Add the dried shrimp, then stir in the shrimp paste, with the soy sauce, lime juice and sugar. Add the chilli and pak choi or spring greens and toss over the heat until the vegetables are just wilted.

4 Transfer the stir-fry to warm individual bowls and serve immediately.

Energy 200Kcal/833kJ; Protein 23.1g; Carbohydrate 6.3g, of which sugars 6.2g; Fat 9.2g, of which saturates 1.7g; Cholesterol 96mg; Calcium 334mg; Fibre 2.4g; Sodium 1223mg.

LEMON GRASS PORK

CHILLIES AND LEMON GRASS FLAVOUR THIS SIMPLE STIR-FRY, WHILE CHOPPED, UNSALTED PEANUTS ADD AN INTERESTING CONTRAST IN TEXTURE. LOOK OUT FOR JARS OF CHOPPED LEMON GRASS, WHICH ARE HANDY WHEN THE FRESH VEGETABLE ISN'T AVAILABLE, AND WILL KEEP IN THE REFRIGERATOR.

SERVES FOUR

INGREDIENTS
   675g/1½lb boneless
      pork loin
   2 lemon grass stalks,
      finely chopped
   4 spring onions (scallions),
      thinly sliced
   5ml/1 tsp salt
   12 black peppercorns,
      coarsely crushed
   30ml/2 tbsp groundnut
      (peanut) oil
   2 garlic cloves, chopped
   2 fresh red chillies, seeded
      and chopped
   5ml/1 tsp soft light brown sugar
   30ml/2 tbsp Thai fish sauce
   25g/1oz/¼ cup roasted unsalted
      peanuts, chopped
   ground black pepper
   coarsely torn coriander (cilantro)
      leaves, to garnish
   cooked rice noodles, to serve

1 Trim any excess fat from the pork. Cut the meat across into 5mm/¼in thick slices, then cut each slice into 5mm/¼in strips. Put the pork into a bowl with the lemon grass, spring onions, salt and crushed peppercorns; mix well. Cover with clear film (plastic wrap) and leave to marinate in a cool place for 30 minutes.

2 Preheat a wok, add the oil and swirl it around. Add the pork mixture and stir-fry over a medium heat for about 3 minutes, until browned all over.

3 Add the garlic and red chillies and stir-fry for a further 5–8 minutes over a medium heat, until the pork is cooked through and tender.

4 Add the sugar, fish sauce and chopped peanuts and toss to mix, then season to taste with black pepper. Serve immediately on a bed of rice noodles, garnished with the coarsely torn coriander leaves.

COOK'S TIP
The most intense heat in chillies is in the membrane surrounding the seeds, so make sure you remove it all.

Energy 297Kcal/1240kJ; Protein 37.9g; Carbohydrate 2.1g, of which sugars 1.7g; Fat 15.2g, of which saturates 3.6g; Cholesterol 106mg; Calcium 20mg; Fibre 0.5g; Sodium 119mg.

CHINESE BRAISED PORK BELLY WITH GREENS

PORK BELLY BECOMES MELTINGLY TENDER IN THIS SLOW-BRAISED DISH FLAVOURED WITH ORANGE, CINNAMON, STAR ANISE AND GINGER. THE FLAVOURS MELD AND MELLOW DURING COOKING TO PRODUCE A RICH, COMPLEX, ROUNDED TASTE. SERVE SIMPLY WITH RICE AND STEAMED GREENS.

SERVES FOUR

INGREDIENTS

    800g/1¾lb pork belly, trimmed
      and cut into 12 pieces
    400ml/14fl oz/1⅔ cups beef stock
    75ml/5 tbsp soy sauce
    finely grated rind and juice
      of 1 large orange
    15ml/1 tbsp finely shredded fresh
      root ginger
    2 garlic cloves, sliced
    15ml/1 tbsp hot chilli powder
    15ml/1 tbsp muscovado sugar
      (molasses)
    3 cinnamon sticks
    3 cloves
    10 black peppercorns
    2–3 star anise
    steamed greens and rice, to serve

1 Place the pork in a wok and pour over water to cover. Bring the water to the boil. Cover, reduce the heat and cook gently for 30 minutes. Drain the pork and return to the wok with the stock, soy sauce, orange rind and juice, ginger, garlic, chilli powder, muscovado sugar, cinnamon sticks, cloves, peppercorns and star anise.

2 Pour over water to just cover the pork belly pieces and cook on a high heat until the mixture comes to a boil.

3 Cover the wok tightly with a lid, then reduce the heat to low and cook gently for 1½ hours, stirring occasionally to prevent the pork from sticking to the base of the wok.

Energy 543Kcal/2260kJ; Protein 38.9g; Carbohydrate 6.6g, of which sugars 6.4g; Fat 40.4g, of which saturates 14.6g; Cholesterol 142mg; Calcium 19mg; Fibre 0g; Sodium 1475mg.

AROMATIC PORK WITH BASIL

THE COMBINATION OF MOIST, JUICY PORK AND MUSHROOMS, CRISP GREEN MANGETOUTS AND FRAGRANT BASIL IN THIS GINGER- AND GARLIC-INFUSED STIR-FRY IS ABSOLUTELY DELICIOUS. SERVED WITH SIMPLE STEAMED JASMINE RICE, IT MAKES A PERFECT QUICK SUPPER DURING THE WEEK.

SERVES FOUR

INGREDIENTS

40g/1½oz cornflour (cornstarch)
500g/1¼lb pork fillet (tenderloin), thinly sliced
15ml/1 tbsp sunflower oil
10ml/2 tsp sesame oil
15ml/1 tbsp very finely shredded fresh root ginger
3 garlic cloves, thinly sliced
200g/7oz mangetouts (snow peas), halved lengthways
300g/11oz/generous 4 cups mixed mushrooms, such as shiitake, button (white) or oyster, sliced if large
120ml/4fl oz/½ cup Chinese cooking wine
45ml/3 tbsp soy sauce
a small handful of sweet basil leaves
salt and ground black pepper
steamed jasmine rice, to serve

1 Place the cornflour in a strong plastic bag. Season well and add the sliced pork. Shake the bag to coat the pork in flour and then remove the pork and shake off any excess flour. Set aside.

2 Preheat the wok over a high heat and add the oils. When very hot, stir in the ginger and garlic and cook for 30 seconds. Add the pork and cook over a high heat for about 5 minutes, stirring often, until sealed.

3 Add the mangetouts and mushrooms to the wok and stir-fry for 2–3 minutes. Add the Chinese cooking wine and soy sauce, stir-fry for 2–3 minutes and remove from the heat.

4 Just before serving, stir the sweet basil leaves into the pork. Serve with steamed jasmine rice.

Energy 298Kcal/1248kJ; Protein 30.4g; Carbohydrate 14.6g, of which sugars 4.8g; Fat 9.8g, of which saturates 2.4g; Cholesterol 79mg; Calcium 41mg; Fibre 2g; Sodium 903mg.

CELLOPHANE NOODLES WITH PORK

SIMPLE, SPEEDY AND SATISFYING, THIS IS THE SORT OF DISH THE WOK WAS MADE FOR. IT LOOKS SPECTACULAR, WITH THE CLEAR, GLASS-LIKE NOODLES CURLING OVER THE COLOURFUL VEGETABLE MIXTURE. A POPULAR THAI DISH, IT IS NOW SERVED ALL OVER THE WORLD.

SERVES TWO

INGREDIENTS

200g/7oz cellophane noodles
30ml/2 tbsp vegetable oil
15ml/1 tbsp magic paste
200g/7oz minced (ground) pork
1 fresh green or red chilli, seeded
  and finely chopped
300g/11oz/3½ cups beansprouts
bunch spring onions (scallions),
  finely chopped
30ml/2 tbsp soy sauce
30ml/2 tbsp Thai fish sauce
30ml/2 tbsp sweet chilli sauce
15ml/1 tbsp palm sugar or light
  muscovado (brown) sugar
30ml/2 tbsp rice vinegar
30ml/2 tbsp roasted peanuts,
  chopped and small bunch fresh
  coriander (cilantro), chopped,
  to garnish

1 Place the noodles in a large bowl, cover with boiling water and soak for 10 minutes. Drain the noodles and set aside until ready to use.

2 Heat the oil in a wok or large, heavy frying pan. Add the magic paste and stir-fry for 2–3 seconds, then add the pork. Stir-fry the meat, breaking it up with a wooden spatula, for 2–3 minutes, until browned all over.

3 Add the chopped chilli to the meat and stir-fry for 3–4 seconds, then add the beansprouts and chopped spring onions, stir-frying for a few seconds after each addition.

4 Snip the noodles into 5cm/2in lengths and add to the wok, with the soy sauce, Thai fish sauce, sweet chilli sauce, sugar and rice vinegar.

5 Toss the ingredients together over the heat until well combined and the noodles have warmed through. Pile on to a platter or into a large bowl. Sprinkle over the peanuts and coriander and serve immediately.

VARIATION
This dish is also very good made with chicken. Replace the pork with the same quantity of minced (ground) chicken.

Energy 755Kcal/3153kJ; Protein 39.8g; Carbohydrate 96.8g, of which sugars 14.6g; Fat 23.3g, of which saturates 4.2g; Cholesterol 63mg; Calcium 94mg; Fibre 4g; Sodium 1158mg.

FIVE-FLAVOUR NOODLES

THE JAPANESE NAME FOR THIS DISH TRANSLATES AS "FIVE DIFFERENT INGREDIENTS"; HOWEVER, THERE'S NOTHING TO STOP YOU ADDING AS MANY DIFFERENT INGREDIENTS AS YOU LIKE TO MAKE AN EXCITING AND TASTY NOODLE STIR-FRY. THE SEASONING MIX IMPARTS A GREAT FLAVOUR.

SERVES FOUR

INGREDIENTS
    300g/11oz dried Chinese thin egg
        noodles or 500g/1¼lb fresh yaki-
        soba noodles
    200g/7oz lean boneless pork,
        thinly sliced
    22ml/4 tsp sunflower oil
    10g/¼oz grated fresh root ginger
    1 garlic clove, crushed
    200g/7oz green cabbage,
        roughly chopped
    115g/4oz/2 cups beansprouts
    1 green (bell) pepper, seeded and cut
        into fine strips
    1 red (bell) pepper, seeded and cut
        into fine strips
    salt and ground black pepper
    20ml/4 tsp ao-nori seaweed, to
        garnish (optional)
For the seasoning mix
    60ml/4 tbsp Worcestershire sauce
    15ml/1 tbsp Japanese soy sauce
    15ml/1 tbsp oyster sauce
    15ml/1 tbsp sugar
    2.5ml/½ tsp salt
    ground white pepper

1 Cook the noodles according to the instructions on the packet. Drain well and set aside.

2 Cut the pork into 3–4cm/1¼–1½in strips and season with salt and pepper.

VARIATION
Try this with strips of tender chicken breast instead of pork.

3 Heat 7.5ml/1½ tsp of the oil in a wok. Stir-fry the pork until just cooked, then remove it from the pan.

4 Wipe the wok with kitchen paper, and heat the remaining oil in it. Add the ginger, garlic and cabbage and stir-fry for 1 minute.

5 Add the beansprouts, stir until softened, then add the peppers and stir-fry for 1 minute more.

6 Return the pork to the pan and add the noodles. Stir in all the ingredients for the seasoning mix and stir-fry for 2–3 minutes. Serve immediately, sprinkled with ao-nori seaweed (if using).

Energy 471Kcal/1988kJ; Protein 22.8g; Carbohydrate 71g, of which sugars 17.4g; Fat 12.6g, of which saturates 3g; Cholesterol 54mg; Calcium 95mg; Fibre 5.2g; Sodium 652mg.

SPICY FRIED NOODLES

THIS IS A WONDERFULLY VERSATILE DISH BECAUSE YOU CAN ADAPT IT TO INCLUDE YOUR FAVOURITE INGREDIENTS — JUST AS LONG AS YOU KEEP A BALANCE OF FLAVOURS, TEXTURES AND COLOURS.

SERVES FOUR

INGREDIENTS

225g/8oz egg thread noodles
60ml/4 tbsp vegetable oil
2 garlic cloves, finely chopped
175g/6oz pork fillet (tenderloin), sliced into thin strips
1 skinless, boneless chicken breast portion (about 175g/6oz), sliced into thin strips
115g/4oz/1 cup cooked peeled prawns (shrimp)
juice of half a lemon
45ml/3 tbsp Thai fish sauce
30ml/2 tbsp soft light brown sugar
2 eggs, beaten
½ fresh red chilli, seeded and finely chopped
50g/2oz/⅔ cup beansprouts
60ml/4 tbsp roasted peanuts, chopped
3 spring onions (scallions), cut into 5cm/2in lengths and shredded
45ml/3 tbsp chopped fresh coriander (cilantro)

1 Bring a large pan of water to the boil. Add the noodles, remove the pan from the heat and leave for 5 minutes.

2 Meanwhile, heat 45ml/3 tbsp of the oil in a wok or large frying pan, add the garlic and cook for 30 seconds. Add the pork and chicken and stir-fry until lightly browned, then add the prawns and stir-fry for 2 minutes.

3 Add the lemon juice, then add the fish sauce and sugar. Stir-fry until the sugar has dissolved.

4 Drain the noodles and add to the wok or pan with the remaining 15ml/1 tbsp oil. Toss all the ingredients together.

5 Pour the beaten eggs over the noodles and stir-fry until almost set, then add the chilli and beansprouts.

6 Divide the roasted peanuts, spring onions and coriander leaves into two equal portions, add one portion to the pan and stir-fry for about 2 minutes.

7 Tip the noodles on to a serving platter. Sprinkle on the remaining roasted peanuts, spring onions and chopped coriander and serve immediately.

COOK'S TIP
Store beansprouts in the refrigerator and use within a day of purchase, as they tend to lose their crispness and become slimy and unpleasant quite quickly. The most commonly used beansprouts are sprouted mung beans, but you could use other types of beansprouts instead.

Energy 597Kcal/2504kJ; Protein 39.3g; Carbohydrate 50.8g, of which sugars 10.3g; Fat 27.8g, of which saturates 5.5g; Cholesterol 226mg; Calcium 76mg; Fibre 2.9g; Sodium 250mg.

NASI GORENG

ONE OF THE MOST POPULAR AND BEST-KNOWN DISHES FROM INDONESIA, THIS IS A MARVELLOUS WAY TO USE UP LEFTOVER RICE, AND MEATS SUCH AS PORK AND CHICKEN.

SERVES FOUR TO SIX

INGREDIENTS
350g/12oz/1¾ cups basmati rice
   (dry weight), cooked and cooled
2 eggs
30ml/2 tbsp water
105ml/7 tbsp sunflower oil
225g/8oz pork fillet or fillet of beef
2–3 fresh red chillies
10ml/2 tsp shrimp paste
2 garlic cloves, crushed
1 onion, sliced
115g/4oz cooked, peeled prawns
   (shrimp)
225g/8oz cooked chicken, chopped
30ml/2 tbsp dark soy sauce
salt and freshly ground black pepper
Deep-fried Onions, to serve

1 Separate the grains of the cooked rice with a fork. Cover and set aside. Beat the eggs with the water and seasoning.

2 Heat 15ml/1 tbsp of the oil in a frying pan or wok, pour in about half the egg mixture and cook until set, without stirring. Roll up the omelette, slide it on to a plate, cut into strips and set aside. Make another omelette in the same way.

3 Cut the pork or beef fillet into neat strips. Finely shred one of the chillies and set aside.

4 Put the shrimp paste into a food processor, add the remaining chilli, garlic and onion. Process to a paste.

5 Heat the remaining oil in a wok. Fry the paste, without browning, until it gives off a spicy aroma.

6 Add the strips of pork or beef and toss the meat over the heat, to seal in the juices. Cook the meat in the wok for about 2 minutes, stirring constantly.

7 Add the prawns, cook for 2 minutes, then add the chicken, rice, and soy sauce, with salt and pepper to taste, stirring constantly. Serve in individual bowls, garnished with omelette strips, shredded chilli and Deep-fried Onions.

Energy 463Kcal/1929kJ; Protein 27.3g; Carbohydrate 49.4g, of which sugars 2.1g; Fat 17.1g, of which saturates 2.7g; Cholesterol 151mg; Calcium 49mg; Fibre 0.5g; Sodium 288mg.

FRAGRANT HARBOUR FRIED RICE

THE CHINESE NAME FOR HONG KONG IS FRAGRANT HARBOUR, AND IT IS THE CROSSROADS FOR MANY STYLES OF COOKING. FRIED RICE IS EVER POPULAR AS YET ANOTHER WAY OF USING UP LITTLE BITS OF THIS AND THAT TO MAKE A VERITABLE FEAST. COOK THE RICE THE DAY BEFORE IF POSSIBLE.

SERVES FOUR

INGREDIENTS

225g/8oz/generous 1 cup long
  grain rice
about 90ml/6 tbsp vegetable oil
2 eggs, beaten
4 Chinese dried mushrooms, soaked
  for 30 minutes in warm water to cover
8 shallots or 2 small onions, sliced
115g/4oz peeled cooked prawns
  (shrimp), thawed if frozen
3 garlic cloves, crushed
115g/4oz cooked pork, cut into
  thin strips
115g/4oz Chinese sausage, cooked
  and sliced at an angle
30ml/2 tbsp light soy sauce
115g/4oz/1 cup frozen peas, thawed
2 spring onions (scallions), shredded
1–2 fresh or dried red chillies,
  seeded (optional)
salt and ground black pepper
coriander (cilantro) leaves, to garnish

1 Bring a large pan of lightly salted water to the boil. Add the rice and cook for 12–15 minutes until just tender. Drain and cool quickly. Tip into a bowl and chill. Ideally use the next day.

2 Heat about 15ml/1 tbsp of the oil in a wok over a medium heat, pour in the beaten eggs and allow to set without stirring. Slide the omelette on to a plate, roll it up and with a sharp knife cut into fine strips. Set aside.

3 Drain the mushrooms, cut off and discard the stems and slice the caps finely. Heat a wok, add 15ml/1 tbsp of the remaining oil and, when hot, stir-fry the shallots or onions until crisp and golden brown. Remove with a slotted spoon and set aside.

4 Add the prawns and garlic to the wok, with a little more oil if needed, and fry for 1 minute.

5 Remove the prawns and garlic from the wok and set aside. Add 15ml/1 tbsp more oil to the wok.

6 Stir-fry the shredded pork and the mushrooms for 2 minutes; add the cooked Chinese sausage slices and heat for a further 2 minutes. Lift out from the wok and keep warm.

7 Wipe the wok, reheat with the remaining oil and stir-fry the rice, adding more oil if needed so the grains are coated. Stir in the soy sauce, salt and pepper, plus half the cooked ingredients.

8 Add the peas and half the spring onions and toss over the heat until the peas are cooked.

9 Pile the fried rice on a heated platter and arrange the remaining cooked ingredients on top, with the remaining spring onions. Add the chilli, if using, and the coriander leaves, to garnish.

COOK'S TIP
There are many theories on the best way to cook rice. This method gives excellent results every time: Put 225g/8oz/ generous 1 cup long grain rice in a sieve and rinse thoroughly in cold water. Place in a large bowl, add salt to taste and pour in just under 600ml/1 pint/2½ cups boiling water. Cover with microwave film, leaving a gap, and cook in a 675 watt microwave on full power for 10 minutes. Leave to stand for 5 minutes more. Cool, then stir with a chopstick.

Energy 450Kcal/1872kJ; Protein 14.5g; Carbohydrate 51g, of which sugars 4.4g; Fat 20.9g, of which saturates 3.1g; Cholesterol 113mg; Calcium 48mg; Fibre 1.1g; Sodium 58mg.

CRISPY THAI NOODLE SALAD

RICE NOODLES PUFF UP AND BECOME LIGHT AND CRISPY WHEN DEEP-FRIED AND MAKE A LOVELY BASE FOR THIS TANGY, FRAGRANT SALAD. SERVE AS A SNACK OR LIGHT MEAL, AND ENJOY THE HEADY COMBINATION OF SPICY CHILLIES, FRAGRANT PORK AND PRAWNS, AND CRISPY NOODLES.

SERVES FOUR

INGREDIENTS

sunflower oil, for deep-frying
115g/4oz rice vermicelli
45ml/3 tbsp groundnut (peanut) oil
2 eggs, lightly beaten with 15ml/
  1 tbsp water
30ml/2 tbsp palm sugar
30ml/2 tbsp Thai fish sauce
15ml/1 tbsp rice wine vinegar
30ml/2 tbsp tomato ketchup
1 fresh red chilli, thinly sliced
3 garlic cloves, crushed
5ml/1 tsp finely grated fresh
  root ginger
200g/7oz minced (ground) pork
400g/14oz cooked peeled tiger
  prawns (shrimp)
4 spring onions (scallions),
  finely shredded
60ml/4 tbsp chopped coriander
  (cilantro) leaves

1 Fill a wok one-third full of sunflower oil and heat to 180°C/350°F or until a cube of bread, dropped into the oil, browns in 45 seconds. Working in batches, deep-fry the vermicelli, for 10–20 seconds, or until puffed up. Remove from the wok with a slotted spoon and drain on kitchen paper.

2 Carefully discard the oil and wipe out the wok. Heat 15ml/1 tbsp of the groundnut oil in the wok. Add half the egg mixture and swirl the wok to make a thin omelette. Cook gently for 2–3 minutes, until the egg has just set and then carefully transfer to a board.

3 Repeat with a further 15ml/1 tbsp of groundnut oil and the remaining egg mixture to make a second omelette. Place the second omelette on top of the first and roll up into a cylinder. Using a sharp knife, cut the cylinder crossways to make thin strips, then set the strips aside on a plate.

4 Mix together the palm sugar, fish sauce, rice wine vinegar, tomato ketchup, chilli, garlic and ginger. Stir half this mixture into the pork and mix.

5 Heat the remaining groundnut oil in the wok. When hot, add the pork mixture and stir-fry for 4–5 minutes until cooked through. Add the prawns and stir-fry for 1–2 minutes.

6 Remove the wok from the heat and add the remaining palm sugar mixture, fried vermicelli, spring onions and coriander and toss to combine.

7 Divide the mixture among four warmed plates and top with the shredded omelette. Serve immediately.

Energy 508Kcal/2118kJ; Protein 35.1g; Carbohydrate 33.1g, of which sugars 10.5g; Fat 26.4g, of which saturates 5g; Cholesterol 371mg; Calcium 142mg; Fibre 0.8g; Sodium 405mg.

SEAFOOD

Some of the finest recipes for the wok feature shellfish and fish, because stir-frying is an ideal method for seafood, which need fast cooking to retain the texture and flavour. The mild flavour of white fish and shellfish is also a perfect foil to the spicy, tangy flavours of Asian cooking. Whether your taste is for a hearty fish dish like Curried Seafood with Coconut Milk or for something with a crisp and crunchy coating, such as Thai Fried Noodles, the wok will prove to be the perfect utensil.

CURRIED SEAFOOD WITH COCONUT MILK

THIS QUICK CURRY IS BASED ON A THAI CLASSIC. THE LOVELY GREEN COLOUR COMES FROM THE FINELY CHOPPED CHILLI AND FRESH HERBS ADDED DURING THE LAST FEW MOMENTS OF COOKING.

SERVES FOUR

INGREDIENTS
225g/8oz small ready-prepared squid
225g/8oz raw tiger prawns
(jumbo shrimp)
400ml/14fl oz/1⅔ cups coconut milk
2 kaffir lime leaves, finely shredded
30ml/2 tbsp Thai fish sauce
450g/1lb firm white fish fillets,
skinned, boned and cut into chunks
2 fresh green chillies, seeded and
finely chopped
30ml/2 tbsp torn fresh basil or
coriander (cilantro) leaves
squeeze of fresh lime juice
cooked Thai jasmine rice,
to serve
For the curry paste
6 spring onions (scallions),
coarsely chopped
4 fresh coriander (cilantro) stems,
coarsely chopped, plus 45ml/3 tbsp
chopped fresh coriander (cilantro)
4 kaffir lime leaves, shredded
8 fresh green chillies, seeded and
coarsely chopped
1 lemon grass stalk,
coarsely chopped
2.5cm/1in piece fresh root ginger,
peeled and coarsely chopped
45ml/3 tbsp chopped fresh basil
15ml/1 tbsp vegetable oil

1 Make the curry paste. Put all the ingredients, except the oil, in a food processor and process to a paste. Alternatively, pound together in a mortar with a pestle. Stir in the oil.

2 Rinse the squid and pat dry with kitchen paper. Cut the bodies into rings and halve the tentacles, if necessary.

3 Heat a wok until hot, add the prawns and stir-fry, without any oil, for about 4 minutes, until they turn pink.

4 Remove the prawns from the wok and leave to cool slightly, then peel off the shells, saving a few with shells on for the garnish. Make a slit along the back of each one and remove the black vein.

5 Pour the coconut milk into the wok, then bring to the boil over a medium heat, stirring constantly. Add 30ml/ 2 tbsp of curry paste, the shredded lime leaves and fish sauce and stir well to mix. Reduce the heat to low and simmer gently for about 10 minutes.

6 Add the squid, prawns and chunks of fish and cook for about 2 minutes, until the seafood is tender. Take care not to overcook the squid as it will become tough very quickly.

7 Just before serving, stir in the chillies and basil or coriander. Taste and adjust the flavour with a squeeze of lime juice. Garnish with prawns in their shells, and serve with Thai jasmine rice.

VARIATIONS
• You can use any firm-fleshed white fish for this curry, such as monkfish, cod, haddock or John Dory.
• If you prefer, you could substitute shelled scallops for the squid. Slice them in half horizontally and add them with the prawns (shrimp). As with the squid, be careful not to overcook them.

Energy 238Kcal/1005kJ; Protein 40.6g; Carbohydrate 7g, of which sugars 6.2g; Fat 5.5g, of which saturates 0.9g; Cholesterol 288mg; Calcium 145mg; Fibre 1.4g; Sodium 622mg.

STIR-FRIED PRAWNS WITH TAMARIND

THIS DISH PERFECTLY ILLUSTRATES HOW VERSATILE THE WOK IS, IT IS USED FIRST FOR DEEP-FRYING, THEN DRY-FRYING THE CHILLIES, AND THEN STIR-FRYING FOR THIS DELICIOUS DISH. LEAVE A FEW PRAWNS IN THEIR SHELLS FOR VISUAL EFFECT.

SERVES FOUR TO SIX

INGREDIENTS
   15ml/1 tbsp chopped garlic
   30ml/2 tbsp sliced shallots
   vegetable oil for deep-frying
   6 dried red chillies
   30ml/2 tbsp vegetable oil
   30ml/2 tbsp chopped onion
   30ml/2 tbsp palm sugar (jaggery) or
      light muscovado (brown) sugar
   30ml/2 tbsp chicken stock or water
   15ml/1 tbsp Thai fish sauce
   90ml/6 tbsp tamarind juice, made
      by mixing tamarind paste with
      warm water
   450g/1lb prawns (shrimp), peeled
   2 spring onions (scallions), chopped,
      to garnish

1 Deep-fry the chopped garlic and sliced shallots, drain on kitchen paper and set aside. Drain the oil from the wok and wipe clean.

2 Add the dried chillies and dry-fry by pressing them against the surface of the wok or pan with a spatula, turning them occasionally. Do not let them burn. Set them aside to cool slightly.

3 Add the oil to the wok or pan and reheat. Add the chopped onion and cook over a medium heat, stirring occasionally, for 2–3 minutes, until softened and golden brown. Add the sugar, stock or water, fish sauce, dry-fried red chillies and the tamarind juice, stirring until the sugar has dissolved.

4 Bring the mixture to the boil, then lower the heat slightly.

5 Add the prawns, and deep-fried garlic and shallots. Toss over the heat for 3–4 minutes, until the prawns are pink and cooked through. Garnish with the spring onions and serve.

Energy 117Kcal/493kJ; Protein 13.6g; Carbohydrate 6.8g, of which sugars 6.4g; Fat 4.2g, of which saturates 0.5g; Cholesterol 146mg; Calcium 69mg; Fibre 0.3g; Sodium 144mg.

CURRIED PRAWNS IN COCONUT MILK

IF YOU USE CANNED COCONUT MILK AND BOUGHT CURRY PASTE, THIS IS ONE OF THE QUICKEST AND EASIEST DISHES THERE IS. SERVED WITH NOODLES, IT MAKES THE PERFECT LIGHT SUPPER FOR A LAZY SUMMER EVENING, OR A QUICK LUNCH RUSTLED UP FROM STORE-CUPBOARD INGREDIENTS.

SERVES FOUR TO SIX

INGREDIENTS
- 600ml/1 pint/2$\frac{1}{2}$ cups coconut milk
- 30ml/2 tbsp yellow curry paste (see below)
- 15ml/1 tbsp Thai fish sauce
- 2.5ml/$\frac{1}{2}$ tsp salt
- 5ml/1 tsp sugar
- 450g/1lb raw king prawns (jumbo shrimp) peeled, thawed if frozen
- 225g/8oz cherry tomatoes
- $\frac{1}{2}$ fresh yellow and orange (bell) pepper, seeded and cut into thin strips, plus chives and juice of $\frac{1}{2}$ lime, to garnish

VARIATION
Use cooked prawns for a quick version of this dish. Add them after the tomatoes and heat through for a minute or two.

1 Put half the coconut milk in a wok or heavy pan and bring to the boil. Add the yellow curry paste, stir until it disperses, then lower the heat and simmer for about 10 minutes.

2 Add the Thai fish sauce, salt, sugar and remaining coconut milk to the sauce. Simmer for 5 minutes more, stirring frequently.

3 Add the prawns and cherry tomatoes. Simmer very gently for about 5 minutes until the prawns are pink and tender.

4 Spoon into a serving dish, sprinkle with lime juice and garnish with the yellow and orange pepper and chives.

COOK'S TIP
To make yellow curry paste, put into a food processor or blender 6–8 fresh yellow chillies, the chopped base of 1 lemon grass stalk, 4 chopped shallots, 4 chopped garlic cloves, 15ml/1 tbsp chopped peeled fresh root ginger, 5ml/1 tsp coriander seeds, 5ml/1 tsp mustard powder, 5ml/1 tsp salt, 2.5ml/$\frac{1}{2}$ tsp ground cinnamon, 15ml/1 tbsp brown sugar and 30ml/2 tbsp sunflower oil. Process to a paste, scrape into a glass jar, cover and keep in the refrigerator.

Energy 99Kcal/421kJ; Protein 13.8g; Carbohydrate 6.9g, of which sugars 6.9g; Fat 2g, of which saturates 0.5g; Cholesterol 146mg; Calcium 92mg; Fibre 0.4g; Sodium 375mg.

FRAGRANT TIGER PRAWNS <u>WITH</u> DILL

THIS ELEGANT DISH HAS A FRESH, LIGHT FLAVOUR AND IS EQUALLY GOOD SERVED AS A SIMPLE SUPPER OR FOR A DINNER PARTY. THE DELICATE TEXTURE OF FRESH PRAWNS GOES REALLY WELL WITH MILD CUCUMBER AND FRAGRANT DILL, AND ALL YOU NEED IS SOME RICE OR NOODLES TO SERVE.

SERVES FOUR TO SIX

INGREDIENTS

500g/1¼lb raw tiger prawns
(jumbo shrimp), heads and shells
removed but tails left on
500g/1¼lb cucumber
30ml/2 tbsp butter
15ml/1 tbsp olive oil
15ml/1 tbsp finely chopped garlic
45ml/3 tbsp chopped fresh dill
juice of 1 lemon
salt and ground black pepper
steamed rice or noodles, to serve

1 Using a small, sharp knife, carefully make a shallow slit along the back of each prawn and use the point of the knife to remove the black vein. Set the prawns aside.

2 Peel the cucumber and slice in half lengthways. Using a small teaspoon, gently scoop out all the seeds and discard. Cut the cucumber into 4 x 1cm/1½ x ½in sticks.

3 Heat a wok over a high heat, then add the butter and oil. When the butter has melted, add the cucumber and garlic and fry over a high heat for 2–3 minutes, stirring continuously.

4 Add the prepared prawns to the wok and continue to stir-fry over a high heat for 3–4 minutes, or until the prawns turn pink and are just cooked through, then remove from the heat.

5 Add the fresh dill and lemon juice to the wok and toss to combine. Season well with salt and ground black pepper and serve immediately with steamed rice or noodles.

Energy 192Kcal/798kJ; Protein 23.2g; Carbohydrate 2.5g, of which sugars 1.9g; Fat 9.8g, of which saturates 4.4g; Cholesterol 260mg; Calcium 123mg; Fibre 0.9g; Sodium 287mg.

SAMBAL GORENG WITH PRAWNS

SAMBAL GORENG IS AN IMMENSELY USEFUL AND ADAPTABLE SAUCE. HERE IT IS USED AS THE BASIS FOR A WOK-COOKED DISH WITH PRAWNS AND GREEN PEPPER, BUT YOU COULD ADD FINE STRIPS OF CALF'S LIVER, CHICKEN LIVERS, TOMATOES, GREEN BEANS OR HARD-BOILED EGGS.

SERVES FOUR TO SIX

INGREDIENTS

350g/12oz peeled cooked prawns (shrimp)
1 green (bell) pepper, seeded and sliced
60ml/4 tbsp tamarind juice
pinch of sugar
45ml/3 tbsp coconut milk or cream
strips of lime rind and red onion slices, to garnish
boiled or steamed rice

For the sambal goreng

2.5cm/1in cube shrimp paste
2 onions, roughly chopped
2 garlic cloves, roughly chopped
2.5cm/1in piece fresh galangal, peeled and sliced
10ml/2 tsp chilli sambal or 2 fresh red chillies, seeded and sliced
1.5ml/¼ tsp salt
30ml/2 tbsp vegetable oil
45ml/3 tbsp tomato purée (paste)
600ml/1 pint/2½ cups vegetable stock or water

2 Heat the oil in a wok or frying pan and fry the paste for 1–2 minutes, without browning, until the mixture gives off a rich aroma. Stir in the tomato purée and the stock or water and cook for 10 minutes. Ladle half the sauce into a bowl and leave to cool. The leftover sauce can be used in another recipe (see Cook's Tip).

3 Add the prawns and green pepper to the remaining sauce. Cook over a medium heat for 3–4 minutes, then stir in the tamarind juice, sugar and coconut milk or cream. Spoon the prawns into warmed serving bowls and garnish with strips of lime rind and sliced red onion. Serve at once with boiled or steamed rice.

1 Make the sambal goreng. Grind the shrimp paste with the onions and garlic using a mortar and pestle. Alternatively, put in a food processor and process to a paste. Add the galangal, chilli sambal or sliced chillies and salt. Process or pound to a fine paste.

COOK'S TIP
Store the remaining sauce in a sealed jar in the refrigerator for up to 3 days or freeze it in a tub for up to 3 months.

Energy 108Kcal/452kJ; Protein 11.8g; Carbohydrate 5.9g, of which sugars 5.1g; Fat 4.3g, of which saturates 0.5g; Cholesterol 118mg; Calcium 72mg; Fibre 1.2g; Sodium 175mg.

GOAN PRAWN CURRY WITH MANGO

THIS SWEET, SPICY, HOT-AND-SOUR CURRY COMES FROM THE SHORES OF WESTERN INDIA. IT IS SIMPLE TO MAKE, AND THE ADDITION OF MANGO AND TAMARIND PRODUCES A VERY FULL, RICH FLAVOUR. IF YOU HAVE TIME, MAKE THE SAUCE THE DAY BEFORE TO GIVE THE FLAVOURS TIME TO DEVELOP.

SERVES FOUR

INGREDIENTS
   5ml/1 tsp hot chilli powder
   15ml/1 tbsp paprika
   2.5ml/½ tsp ground turmeric
   4 garlic cloves, crushed
   10ml/2 tsp finely grated ginger
   30ml/2 tbsp ground coriander
   10ml/2 tsp ground cumin
   15ml/1 tbsp palm sugar (jaggery)
   1 green mango
   400g/14oz can coconut milk
   10ml/2 tsp salt
   15ml/1 tbsp tamarind paste
   1kg/2¼lb large prawns (shrimp)
   chopped coriander (cilantro),
   to garnish
   steamed white rice, chopped tomato,
   cucumber and onion salad, to serve

VARIATION
Peel the prawns before cooking if you like, but be careful not to overcook.

1 Wash, stone and slice the mango and set aside. In a large bowl, combine the chilli powder, paprika, turmeric, garlic, ginger, ground coriander, ground cumin and jaggery or palm sugar. Add 400ml/14fl oz/1⅔ cups cold water to the bowl and stir to combine.

2 Pour the spice mixture into a wok and place over a high heat and bring the mixture to the boil. Cover the wok with a lid, reduce the heat to low and simmer gently for 8–10 minutes.

3 Add the mango, coconut milk, salt and tamarind paste to the wok and stir to combine. Bring to a simmer and then add the prawns.

4 Cover the wok and cook gently for 10–12 minutes, or until the prawns have turned pink and are cooked.

5 Serve the curry garnished with chopped coriander, accompanied by steamed white rice and a tomato, cucumber and onion salad.

Energy 151Kcal/648kJ; Protein 22.1g; Carbohydrate 14.1g, of which sugars 14g; Fat 1.1g, of which saturates 0.5g; Cholesterol 263mg; Calcium 143mg; Fibre 1g; Sodium 2102mg.

HERB- AND CHILLI-SEARED SCALLOPS

TENDER, SUCCULENT SCALLOPS TASTE SIMPLY DIVINE WHEN MARINATED IN FRESH CHILLI, FRAGRANT MINT AND AROMATIC BASIL, THEN QUICKLY SEARED IN A PIPING HOT WOK. IF YOU CAN'T FIND KING SCALLOPS FOR THIS RECIPE, USE TWICE THE QUANTITY OF SMALLER QUEEN SCALLOPS.

SERVES FOUR

INGREDIENTS
20–24 king scallops, cleaned
120ml/4fl oz/½ cup olive oil
finely grated rind and juice
   of 1 lemon
30ml/2 tbsp finely chopped mixed
   fresh mint and basil
1 fresh red chilli, seeded and
   finely chopped
salt and ground black pepper
500g/1¼lb pak choi (bok choy)

1 Place the scallops in a shallow, non-metallic bowl in a single layer. In a clean bowl, mix together half the oil, the lemon rind and juice, chopped herbs and chilli and spoon over the scallops. Season well with salt and black pepper, cover and set aside.

2 Using a sharp knife, cut each pak choi lengthways into four pieces.

VARIATION
If you can't find pak choi (bok choy) use Chinese broccoli, purple sprouting broccoli or Swiss chard instead.

3 Heat a wok over a high heat. When hot, drain the scallops (reserving the marinade) and add to the wok. Cook for 1 minute on each side, or until cooked to your liking.

4 Pour the marinade over the scallops and remove the wok from the heat. Transfer the scallops and juices to a platter and keep warm. Wipe out the wok with a piece of kitchen paper.

5 Place the wok over a high heat. When all traces of moisture have evaporated, add the remaining oil. When the oil is hot add the pak choi and stir-fry over a high heat for 2–3 minutes, until the leaves wilt.

6 Divide the greens among four warmed serving plates, then top with the reserved scallops and their juices and serve immediately.

Energy 410Kcal/1714kJ; Protein 44.5g; Carbohydrate 8.3g, of which sugars 2.1g; Fat 22.3g, of which saturates 3.5g; Cholesterol 82mg; Calcium 286mg; Fibre 3.2g; Sodium 494mg.

SPICED SCALLOPS AND SUGAR SNAP PEAS ON CRISPY NOODLE CAKES

TENDER, JUICY SCALLOPS AND SUGAR SNAP PEAS COOKED IN SPICES AND SERVED ON A BED OF FRIED NOODLES IS A WINNING COMBINATION. IT'S SIMPLE AND STYLISH AND MAKES A GREAT DISH FOR SPECIAL-OCCASION ENTERTAINING.

SERVES FOUR

INGREDIENTS
  45ml/3 tbsp oyster sauce
  10ml/2 tsp soy sauce
  5ml/1 tsp sesame oil
  5ml/1 tsp golden caster
   (superfine) sugar
  30ml/2 tbsp sunflower oil
  2 fresh red chillies, finely sliced
  4 garlic cloves, finely chopped
  10ml/2 tsp finely chopped fresh
   root ginger
  250g/9oz sugar snap peas, trimmed
  500g/1¼lb king scallops, cleaned,
   roes discarded and sliced in half
  3 spring onions (scallions),
   finely shredded
For the noodle cakes
  250g/9oz fresh thin egg noodles
  10ml/2 tsp sesame oil
  120ml/4fl oz/½ cup sunflower oil

1 Cook the noodles in a wok of boiling water for 1 minute, or until tender. Drain well and transfer to a bowl with the sesame oil and 15ml/1 tbsp of the sunflower oil. Spread the noodles out on a large baking sheet and leave to dry in a warm place for 1 hour.

VARIATION
Use king prawns (jumbo shrimp) instead of scallops, if you like.

2 To cook the noodles, heat 15ml/ 1 tbsp of the oil in a non-stick wok over a high heat. Divide the noodle mixture into four portions and add one portion to the wok. Using a spatula, flatten it out and shape it into a cake.

3 Reduce the heat slightly and cook the cake for about 5 minutes on each side, or until crisp and golden. Drain on kitchen paper and keep warm while you make the remaining three noodle cakes in the same way.

4 Mix together the oyster sauce, soy sauce, sesame oil and sugar in a small bowl, stirring until the sugar has dissolved completely.

5 Heat a wok over medium heat and add the sunflower oil. When hot add the chillies, garlic and ginger, and stir-fry for 30 seconds. Add the sugar snap peas and stir-fry for 1–2 minutes.

6 Add the scallops and spring onions to the wok and stir fry over high heat for 1 minute. Stir in the oyster sauce mixture and cook for a further 1 minute until warmed through.

7 To serve, place a noodle cake on each of four warmed plates and top each one with the scallop mixture. Serve immediately.

Energy 689Kcal/2888kJ; Protein 41.4g; Carbohydrate 59.9g, of which sugars 6.2g; Fat 33.3g, of which saturates 5.4g; Cholesterol 78mg; Calcium 73mg; Fibre 5g; Sodium 700mg.

LAKSA LEMAK

THIS SPICY SOUP MAKES A MARVELLOUS PARTY DISH, AND IS SUBSTANTIAL ENOUGH FOR AN ENTIRE MAIN COURSE. GUESTS SPOON NOODLES INTO WIDE SOUP BOWLS, ADD ACCOMPANIMENTS OF THEIR CHOICE, TOP UP WITH SOUP AND THEN TAKE A FEW PRAWN CRACKERS TO NIBBLE.

SERVES SIX

INGREDIENTS

675g/1½lb small clams
50g/2oz ikan bilis (dried anchovies)
2 × 400ml/14fl oz cans coconut milk
900ml/1½ pints/3¾ cups water
115g/4oz shallots, finely chopped
4 garlic cloves, chopped
6 macadamia nuts or blanched
  almonds, chopped
3 lemon grass stalks, root trimmed
90ml/6 tbsp sunflower oil
1cm/½in cube shrimp paste
25g/1oz/¼ cup mild curry powder
a few curry leaves
2–3 aubergines (eggplants), trimmed
675g/1½lb raw peeled prawns
  (shrimp)
10ml/2 tsp sugar
1 head Chinese leaves (Chinese
  cabbage), thinly sliced
115g/4oz/2 cups beansprouts, rinsed
2 spring onions (scallions), finely
  chopped
50g/2oz crispy fried onions
115g/4oz fried tofu
675g/1½lb mixed noodles
prawn (shrimp) crackers, to serve

1 Scrub the clams and then put in a large pan with 1cm/½in water. Bring to the boil, cover and steam for 3–4 minutes until all the the clams have opened. Drain.

2 Put the ikan bilis (dried anchovies) in a pan and add the water. Bring to the boil and simmer for 20 minutes.

3 Make up the coconut milk to 1.2 litres/2 pints/5 cups with water.

4 Meanwhile, put the shallots, garlic and nuts into a mortar. Cut off the lower 5cm/2in of two of the lemon grass stalks, chop finely and add to the mortar. Pound the mixture to a paste.

5 Heat the oil in a wok, add the shallot paste and fry until the mixture gives off a rich aroma. Bruise the remaining lemon grass stalk and add to the pan. Toss over the heat to release its flavour.

6 Mix the shrimp paste and curry powder to a paste with a little of the coconut milk, add to the wok and toss the mixture over the heat for 1 minute, stirring all the time, and keeping the heat low. Stir in the remaining coconut milk. Add the curry leaves and leave the mixture to simmer while you prepare the accompaniments.

7 Strain the ikan bilis, retaining the stock. Discard the ikan bilis and return the stock to the pan, bring to the boil, then add the whole aubergines. Cook for about 10 minutes or until the flesh is tender and the skins can be removed with ease.

COOK'S TIP
Dried shrimp or prawn paste, also called blachan, is sold in small blocks and is available from Asian supermarkets.

8 Lift the aubergines out of the pan of stock, peel, discard the skin, and cut the flesh into thick strips. Arrange the aubergines on a serving platter.

9 Sprinkle the prawns with sugar, add to the stock pan and cook for 2–4 minutes until they turn pink. Remove and place next to the aubergines. Gradually stir the remaining ikan bilis stock into the pan of soup and bring to the boil.

10 Place the clams, Chinese leaves, beansprouts, spring onions and crispy fried onions on the platter.

11 Rinse the fried tofu in boiling water, cool slightly and squeeze to remove excess oil. Cut each piece in half and add to the soup. Lower the heat to a very gentle simmer.

12 Cook the noodles according to the instructions, drain and pile in a dish. Remove the curry leaves and lemon grass from the soup.

13 Place the noodles, soup and the platter of seafood and vegetables on the table, along with a bowl of prawn crackers. Guests can then help themselves to what they want.

VARIATION
You could substitute mussels for clams, if you like. Scrub them thoroughly, removing any beards, and cook them in lightly salted water until they open. As when preparing the clams, discard any mussels that remain closed.

Energy 814Kcal/3432kJ; Protein 51.2g; Carbohydrate 101.8g, of which sugars 16.6g; Fat 25.2g, of which saturates 2.2g; Cholesterol 258mg; Calcium 558mg; Fibre 7.7g; Sodium 1302mg.

THAI FRIED NOODLES

THIS TASTY DISH IS OFTEN SERVED FOR BREAKFAST IN THAILAND, SO IF YOU FANCY AN EARLY MORNING WORKOUT WITH A WOK, GIVE IT A TRY. IT ALSO MAKES A GREAT SUPPER.

SERVES FOUR TO SIX

INGREDIENTS

    16 raw tiger prawns (jumbo shrimp)
    350g/12oz rice noodles
    45ml/3 tbsp vegetable oil
    15ml/1 tbsp chopped garlic
    2 eggs, lightly beaten
    15ml/1 tbsp dried
      shrimp, rinsed
    30ml/2 tbsp pickled
      mooli (daikon)
    50g/2oz fried tofu, cut into
      small slivers
    2.5ml/½ tsp dried chilli flakes
    1 large bunch garlic chives,
      about 115g/4oz, cut into
      5cm/2in lengths
    225g/8oz/4 cups beansprouts
    50g/2oz/½ cup roasted peanuts,
      coarsely ground
    5ml/1 tsp granulated sugar
    15ml/1 tbsp dark soy sauce
    30ml/2 tbsp Thai fish sauce
    30ml/2 tbsp tamarind juice, made
      by mixing tamarind paste with
      warm water
    fresh coriander (cilantro) leaves and
      lime wedges to garnish

1 Peel the prawns, leaving the tails intact. Carefully cut along the back of each prawn and remove the dark vein.

2 Place the rice noodles in a large bowl, add warm water to cover and leave to soak for 20–30 minutes, then drain thoroughly and set aside.

3 Heat 15ml/1 tbsp of the oil in a wok. Stir-fry the garlic until golden. Stir in the prawns and cook for 1–2 minutes, until pink. Remove and set aside.

4 Heat 15ml/1 tbsp of the remaining oil in the wok. Add the eggs and tilt the wok to make a thin layer. Stir to scramble and break up. Remove from the wok and set aside with the prawns.

5 Heat the remaining oil in the same wok. Add the dried shrimp, pickled mooli, tofu slivers and dried chilli flakes. Stir briefly. Add the noodles and stir-fry for about 5 minutes.

6 Add the garlic chives, half the beansprouts and half the peanuts. Add the granulated sugar, then season with soy sauce, fish sauce and tamarind juice. Mix well and cook until the noodles are heated through.

7 Return the prawn and egg mixture to the wok and mix with the noodles. Serve topped with the remaining beansprouts and peanuts, and garnished with the coriander leaves and lime wedges.

COOK'S TIP

There are numerous species of prawns (shrimp) and they range in colour from black to white, although most turn pink when cooked. Genuine Indo-Pacific tiger prawns, of which there are several types, have a fine flavour and a good texture. They grow up to 28cm/11in in length. However, not all large, warm-water varieties are so succulent, and even farmed prawns tend to be quite expensive.

Energy 372Kcal/1553kJ; Protein 14.2g; Carbohydrate 51.1g, of which sugars 2.3g; Fat 11.6g, of which saturates 2g; Cholesterol 128mg; Calcium 57mg; Fibre 1.1g; Sodium 274mg.

FRIED JASMINE RICE WITH PRAWNS

STRIPS OF OMELETTE ARE USED TO GARNISH THIS RICE DISH. USE YOUR WOK FOR FRYING THE OMELETTE — THE SLOPING SIDES MAKE IT EASY TO SPREAD THE BEATEN EGG THINLY AND THEN TO SLIDE IT OUT, READY FOR ROLLING AND SLICING.

SERVES FOUR TO SIX

INGREDIENTS

   45ml/3 tbsp vegetable oil
   1 egg, beaten
   1 onion, chopped
   15ml/1 tbsp chopped garlic
   15ml/1 tbsp shrimp paste
   1kg/2¼lb/4 cups cooked jasmine rice
   350g/12oz cooked shelled prawns
   (shrimp)
   50g/2oz thawed frozen peas
   oyster sauce, to taste
   2 spring onions (scallions), chopped
   15–20 Thai basil leaves, roughly
    snipped, plus an extra sprig,
    to garnish

1 Heat 15ml/1 tbsp of the oil in a wok or frying pan. Add the beaten egg and swirl it around to set like a thin pancake.

2 Cook the pancake (on one side only) over a gentle heat until golden. Slide the pancake on to a board, roll up and cut into thin strips. Set aside.

3 Heat the remaining oil in the wok or pan, add the onion and garlic and stir-fry for 2–3 minutes. Stir in the shrimp paste and mix well until thoroughly combined.

4 Add the rice, prawns and peas and toss and stir together, until everything is heated through.

5 Season with oyster sauce to taste, taking great care as the shrimp paste is salty. Mix in the spring onions and basil leaves. Transfer to a serving dish and top with the strips of egg pancake. Serve, garnished with a sprig of basil.

Energy 357Kcal/1508kJ; Protein 17.6g; Carbohydrate 54.6g, of which sugars 1.7g; Fat 9.2g, of which saturates 1.5g; Cholesterol 154mg; Calcium 111mg; Fibre 1g; Sodium 198mg.

CRAB AND TOFU STIR-FRY

FOR A LIGHT MEAL SUITABLE FOR SERVING AT ANY TIME, THIS SPEEDY STIR-FRY IS THE IDEAL CHOICE. AS YOU NEED ONLY A LITTLE CRAB MEAT — AND YOU COULD USE THE CANNED VARIETY — THIS IS A VERY ECONOMICAL DISH. THE TOFU BOOSTS THE PROTEIN CONTENT.

SERVES TWO

INGREDIENTS
- 250g/9oz silken tofu
- 60ml/4 tbsp vegetable oil
- 2 garlic cloves, finely chopped
- 115g/4oz white crab meat
- 130g/4½oz/generous 1 cup baby corn, halved lengthways
- 2 spring onions (scallions), chopped
- 1 fresh red chilli, seeded and finely chopped
- 30ml/2 tbsp soy sauce
- 15ml/1 tbsp Thai fish sauce
- 5ml/1 tsp palm sugar (jaggery) or light muscovado (brown) sugar
- juice of 1 lime
- small bunch fresh coriander (cilantro), chopped, to garnish

1 Using a sharp knife, cut the silken tofu into 1cm/½in cubes.

2 Heat the oil in a wok or large, heavy frying pan. Add the tofu cubes and stir-fry until golden all over, taking care not to break them up. Remove the tofu with a slotted spoon and set aside.

3 Add the garlic to the wok or pan and stir-fry until golden. Add the crab meat, tofu, corn, spring onions, chilli, soy sauce, fish sauce and sugar. Cook, stirring constantly, until the vegetables are just tender. Stir in the lime juice, transfer to warmed bowls, sprinkle with the coriander and serve immediately.

Energy 365Kcal/1514kJ; Protein 23.1g; Carbohydrate 5.8g, of which sugars 4.8g; Fat 27.9g, of which saturates 3.3g; Cholesterol 41mg; Calcium 719mg; Fibre 1.2g; Sodium 2131mg.

SPICED HALIBUT AND TOMATO CURRY AND GINGER

THE CHUNKY CUBES OF WHITE FISH CONTRAST VISUALLY WITH THE RICH RED SPICY TOMATO SAUCE AND TASTE JUST AS GOOD AS THEY LOOK. HALIBUT IS USED HERE, BUT YOU CAN USE ANY TYPE OF FIRM WHITE FISH FOR THIS RECIPE.

SERVES FOUR

INGREDIENTS

    1 lemon
    60ml/4 tbsp rice wine vinegar
    30ml/2 tbsp cumin seeds
    5ml/1 tsp ground turmeric
    5ml/1 tsp chilli powder
    5ml/1 tsp salt
    750g/1lb 11oz thick halibut
      fillets, skinned and cubed
    60ml/4 tbsp sunflower oil
    1 onion, finely chopped
    3 garlic cloves, finely grated
    30ml/2 tbsp finely grated
      fresh root ginger
    10ml/2 tsp black mustard seeds
    2 x 400g/14oz cans
      chopped tomatoes
    5ml/1 tsp sugar
    chopped coriander (cilantro)
      and sliced fresh green chilli,
      to garnish
    natural (plain) yogurt,
      to drizzle (optional)
    basmati rice, pickles and
      poppadums, to serve

1 Squeeze the lemon and pour 60ml/4tbsp of the juice into a shallow glass bowl. Add the vinegar, cumin, turmeric, chilli powder and salt.

2 Add the cubed fish to the bowl and coat evenly. Cover the bowl with clear film (plastic wrap) and refrigerate for 25–30 minutes.

3 Meanwhile, heat a wok over a high heat and add the oil. When hot, add the onion, garlic, ginger and mustard seeds. Reduce the heat to low and cook very gently for about 10 minutes, stirring occasionally.

4 Add the tomatoes and sugar to the wok, bring to the boil, reduce the heat, cover and cook gently for 15–20 minutes, stirring occasionally.

5 Add the fish and its marinade to the wok, stir gently to mix, then cover and simmer gently for 15–20 minutes, or until the fish is cooked through and flakes easily with a fork.

6 Ladle the curry into shallow bowls, garnish with fresh coriander and green chillies, and drizzle over some natural yogurt if you like. Serve with basmati rice, pickles and poppadums.

COOK'S TIP
Halibut is quite a dense fish, so will take about 15 minutes to cook, especially if the cubes are thick. It is important not to overcook the fish, so if you choose a different type, or buy fillets that are relatively thin, check after 5 minutes. As soon as the flesh becomes opaque and the fish flakes easily when prodded with a fork or the tip of a knife, it is ready.

Energy 335Kcal/1409kJ; Protein 41.9g; Carbohydrate 8.4g, of which sugars 8.1g; Fat 15.2g, of which saturates 2.1g; Cholesterol 66mg; Calcium 73mg; Fibre 2.2g; Sodium 622mg.

VEGETARIAN MAIN DISHES

The recipes in this section are exciting and innovative without being overly intricate. Aromatic Okra and Coconut Stir-fry, for instance, tastes spectacular, is easy to cook at home, and only takes about 10 minutes. Other unusual offerings are Sweet Pumpkin and Peanut Curry and Thai Noodles with Chinese Chives. A few recipes in this chapter contain Thai fish sauce, so if you or your guests do not eat fish, as well as meat, you will need to substitute the fish sauce with the same amount of mushroom ketchup.

SWEET PUMPKIN AND PEANUT CURRY

A HEARTY, SOOTHING CURRY PERFECT FOR AUTUMN OR WINTER EVENINGS. ITS CHEERFUL COLOUR ALONE WILL RAISE THE SPIRITS — AND THE COMBINATION OF PUMPKIN AND PEANUTS TASTES GREAT.

SERVES FOUR

INGREDIENTS

    30ml/2 tbsp vegetable oil
    4 garlic cloves, crushed
    4 shallots, finely chopped
    30ml/2 tbsp yellow curry paste
    600ml/1 pint/2½ cups
      vegetable stock
    2 kaffir lime leaves, torn
    15ml/1 tbsp chopped fresh galangal
    450g/1lb pumpkin, peeled, seeded
      and diced
    225g/8oz sweet potatoes, diced
    90g/3½oz/scant 1 cup unsalted,
      roasted peanuts, chopped
    300ml/½ pint/1¼ cups coconut milk
    90g/3½oz/1½ cups chestnut
      mushrooms, sliced
    30ml/2 tbsp soy sauce
    50g/2oz/⅓ cup pumpkin
      seeds, toasted, and fresh green
      chilli flowers, to garnish

1 Heat the oil in a wok. Add the garlic and shallots and cook over a medium heat, stirring occasionally, for 10 minutes, until softened and golden. Do not let them burn.

2 Add the yellow curry paste and stir-fry over medium heat for 30 seconds, until fragrant, then add the stock, lime leaves, galangal, pumpkin and sweet potatoes. Bring to the boil, stirring frequently, then reduce the heat to low and simmer gently for 15 minutes.

3 Add the peanuts, coconut milk and mushrooms. Stir in the soy sauce and simmer for 5 minutes more. Spoon into warmed individual serving bowls, garnish with the pumpkin seeds and chillies and serve.

COOK'S TIP
The well-drained vegetables from any of these curries would make a very tasty filling for a pastry or pie. This may not be a Thai tradition, but it is a good example of fusion food.

Energy 285Kcal/1189kJ; Protein 8.5g; Carbohydrate 24.8g, of which sugars 12.8g; Fat 17.5g, of which saturates 3g; Cholesterol 0mg; Calcium 94mg; Fibre 4.9g; Sodium 535mg.

TOFU AND GREEN BEAN RED CURRY

RED CURRY PASTE IS ONE OF THE AUTHENTIC FLAVOURINGS OF THAI COOKING, AND WORKS JUST AS WELL IN VEGETARIAN DISHES AS IT DOES IN MEAT-BASED RECIPES.

SERVES FOUR TO SIX

INGREDIENTS
    600ml/1 pint/2½ cups coconut milk
    15ml/1 tbsp Thai red curry paste
    45ml/3 tbsp Thai fish sauce or
      mushroom ketchup
    10ml/2 tsp palm sugar (jaggery) or
      light muscovado (brown) sugar
    225g/8oz/3¼ cups button
      (white) mushrooms
    115g/4oz/scant 1 cup green
      beans, trimmed
    175g/6oz firm tofu, rinsed, drained
      and cut in 2cm/¾in cubes
    4 kaffir lime leaves, torn
    2 fresh red chillies, sliced
    fresh coriander (cilantro) leaves,
      to garnish

1 Pour about one-third of the coconut milk into a wok. Cook until it starts to separate and an oily sheen appears on the surface.

2 Add the red curry paste, fish sauce or mushroom ketchup and sugar to the wok. Mix thoroughly, then add the mushrooms. Stir and cook for 1 minute.

3 Stir in the remaining coconut milk. Bring back to the boil, then add the green beans and tofu cubes. Simmer gently for 4–5 minutes more.

4 Stir in the kaffir lime leaves and sliced red chillies. Spoon the curry into a serving dish, garnish with the coriander leaves and serve immediately.

Energy 79Kcal/333kJ; Protein 3.9g; Carbohydrate 8.2g, of which sugars 7.8g; Fat 3.6g, of which saturates 0.6g; Cholesterol 0mg; Calcium 189mg; Fibre 0.8g; Sodium 647mg.

THAI YELLOW VEGETABLE CURRY

THIS HOT AND SPICY CURRY MADE WITH COCONUT MILK HAS A CREAMY RICHNESS THAT CONTRASTS WONDERFULLY WITH THE HEAT OF CHILLI AND THE BITE OF LIGHTLY COOKED VEGETABLES.

SERVES FOUR

INGREDIENTS
    30ml/2 tbsp sunflower oil
    200ml/7fl oz/scant 1 cup
      coconut cream
    300ml/½ pint/1¼ cups coconut milk
    150ml/¼ pint/⅔ cup vegetable
      stock
    200g/7oz snake beans, cut into
      2cm/¾in lengths
    200g/7oz baby corn
    4 baby courgettes (zucchini), sliced
    1 small aubergine (eggplant), cubed
      or sliced
    10ml/2 tsp palm sugar (jaggery)
    fresh coriander (cilantro) leaves,
      to garnish
    noodles or rice, to serve
For the curry paste
    10ml/2 tsp hot chilli powder
    10ml/2 tsp ground coriander
    10ml/2 tsp ground cumin
    5ml/1 tsp ground turmeric
    15ml/1 tbsp chopped fresh
      galangal
    10ml/2 tsp finely grated garlic
    30ml/2 tbsp finely chopped
      lemon grass
    4 red Asian shallots, finely
      chopped
    5ml/1 tsp finely chopped lime rind

1 Make the curry paste. Place the spices, galangal, garlic, lemon grass, shallots and lime rind in a small food processor and blend with 30–45ml/2–3 tbsp of cold water to make a smooth paste. Add a little more water if the paste seems too dry.

2 Heat a large wok over a medium heat and add the sunflower oil. When hot add 30–45ml/2–3 tbsp of the curry paste and stir-fry for 1–2 minutes. Add the coconut cream and cook gently for 8–10 minutes, or until the mixture starts to separate.

3 Add the coconut milk, stock and vegetables and cook gently for 8–10 minutes, until the vegetables are just tender. Stir in the palm sugar, garnish with coriander leaves and serve with noodles or rice.

COOK'S TIP
To make your own curry paste you will need a good food processor or blender, preferably one with an attachment for processing smaller quantities. Alternatively, you can use a large mortar and pestle, but be warned – it will be hard work. Store any remaining curry paste in a screw-top jar in the refrigerator for up to a week.

Energy 126Kcal/528kJ; Protein 4.7g; Carbohydrate 12.7g, of which sugars 11.9g; Fat 6.7g, of which saturates 1.1g; Cholesterol 5mg; Calcium 90mg; Fibre 2.5g; Sodium 752mg.

CORN <u>AND</u> CASHEW NUT CURRY

A SUBSTANTIAL CURRY, DUE TO THE POTATOES AND CORN, THIS COMBINES ALL THE ESSENTIAL FLAVOURS OF SOUTHERN THAILAND. IT IS DELICIOUSLY AROMATIC, BUT THE FLAVOUR IS FAIRLY MILD.

SERVES FOUR

INGREDIENTS
- 30ml/2 tbsp vegetable oil
- 4 shallots, chopped
- 90g/3½oz/scant 1 cup cashew nuts
- 5ml/1 tsp Thai red curry paste
- 400g/14oz potatoes, peeled and cut into chunks
- 1 lemon grass stalk, finely chopped
- 200g/7oz can chopped tomatoes
- 600ml/1 pint/2½ cups boiling water
- 200g/7oz/generous 1 cup drained canned whole kernel corn
- 4 celery sticks, sliced
- 2 kaffir lime leaves, rolled into cylinders and thinly sliced
- 15ml/1 tbsp tomato ketchup
- 15ml/1 tbsp light soy sauce
- 5ml/1 tsp palm sugar (jaggery) or light muscovado (brown) sugar
- 4 spring onions (scallions), thinly sliced
- small bunch fresh basil, chopped

COOK'S TIP
Rolling the lime leaves into cylinders before slicing with a sharp knife produces very fine strips – a technique known as cutting *en chiffonnade*. Remove the central rib from the leaves before cutting them.

1 Heat the oil in a wok. Add the shallots and stir-fry over a medium heat for 2–3 minutes, until softened. Add the cashew nuts and stir-fry for a few minutes until they are golden.

2 Stir in the red curry paste. Stir-fry for 1 minute, then add the potatoes, lemon grass, tomatoes and boiling water.

3 Bring back to the boil, then reduce the heat to low, cover and simmer gently for 15–20 minutes, or until the potatoes are tender.

4 Stir the corn, celery, lime leaves, ketchup, soy sauce, sugar and spring onions into the pan or wok. Simmer for a further 5 minutes, until heated through, then spoon into warmed serving bowls. Sprinkle with the sliced spring onions and basil and serve.

Energy 401Kcal/1681kJ; Protein 9.9g; Carbohydrate 51.7g, of which sugars 16.3g; Fat 18.6g, of which saturates 3.2g; Cholesterol 0mg; Calcium 41mg; Fibre 3.9g; Sodium 698mg.

AROMATIC OKRA AND COCONUT STIR-FRY

STIR-FRIED OKRA SPICED WITH MUSTARD, CUMIN AND RED CHILLIES AND SPRINKLED WITH FRESHLY GRATED COCONUT MAKES A GREAT QUICK SUPPER. IT IS THE PERFECT WAY TO ENJOY THESE SUCCULENT PODS, WITH THE SWEETNESS OF THE COCONUT COMPLEMENTING THE WARM SPICES.

SERVES FOUR

INGREDIENTS
600g/1lb 6oz okra
60ml/4 tbsp sunflower oil
1 onion, finely chopped
15ml/1 tbsp mustard seeds
15ml/1 tbsp cumin seeds
2–3 dried red chillies
10–12 curry leaves
2.5ml/½ tsp ground turmeric
90g/3½ oz freshly grated coconut
salt and ground black pepper
poppadums, rice or naan, to serve

1 With a sharp knife, cut each of the okra diagonally into 1cm/½ in lengths. Set aside. Heat the wok and add the sunflower oil.

2 When the oil is hot add the chopped onion and stir-fry over a medium heat for about 5 minutes until softened.

3 Add the mustard seeds, cumin seeds, red chillies and curry leaves to the onions and stir-fry over a high heat for about 2 minutes.

4 Add the okra and turmeric to the wok and continue to stir-fry over a high heat for 3–4 minutes.

5 Remove the wok from the heat, sprinkle over the coconut and season well with salt and ground black pepper. Serve immediately with poppadums, steamed rice or naan bread.

COOK'S TIP
Fresh okra is widely available from most supermarkets and Asian stores. Choose fresh, firm, green specimens and avoid any that are limp or turning brown.

Energy 211Kcal/873kJ; Protein 5g; Carbohydrate 6.3g, of which sugars 5.2g; Fat 18.7g, of which saturates 7.1g; Cholesterol 0mg; Calcium 246mg; Fibre 7.6g; Sodium 15mg.

STIR-FRIED SEEDS AND VEGETABLES

THE CONTRAST BETWEEN THE CRUNCHY SEEDS AND VEGETABLES AND THE RICH, SAVOURY SAUCE IS WHAT MAKES THIS DISH SO DELICIOUS. SUPER-SPEEDY WHEN TOSSED TOGETHER IN THE WOK, IT CAN BE SERVED ON ITS OWN, OR WITH RICE OR NOODLES.

SERVES FOUR

INGREDIENTS
- 30ml/2 tbsp vegetable oil
- 30ml/2 tbsp sesame seeds
- 30ml/2 tbsp sunflower seeds
- 30ml/2 tbsp pumpkin seeds
- 2 garlic cloves, finely chopped
- 2.5cm/1in piece fresh root ginger, peeled and finely chopped
- 2 large carrots, cut into batons
- 2 large courgettes (zucchini), cut into batons
- 90g/3½oz/1½ cups oyster mushrooms, broken in pieces
- 150g/5oz watercress or spinach leaves, coarsely chopped
- small bunch fresh mint or coriander (cilantro), leaves and stems chopped
- 60ml/4 tbsp black bean sauce
- 30ml/2 tbsp light soy sauce
- 15ml/1 tbsp palm sugar (jaggery) or light muscovado (brown) sugar
- 30ml/2 tbsp rice vinegar

1 Heat the oil in a wok. Add the seeds. Toss over a medium heat for 1 minute, then add the garlic and ginger and continue to stir-fry until the ginger is aromatic and the garlic is golden. Do not let the spices or garlic burn or they will taste bitter.

2 Add the carrot and courgette batons and the mushroom pieces to the wok and stir-fry over a medium heat for a further 5 minutes, or until all the vegetables are crisp-tender and are golden at the edges.

3 Add the watercress or spinach with the fresh herbs. Toss over the heat for 1 minute, then stir in the black bean sauce, soy sauce, sugar and vinegar. Stir-fry for 1–2 minutes, until combined and hot. Serve immediately.

COOK'S TIP
Oyster mushrooms have acquired their name because of their texture, rather than flavour, which is quite superb. They are delicate, so it is usually better to tear them into pieces along the lines of the gills, rather than slice them with a knife.

Energy 211Kcal/873kJ; Protein 5g; Carbohydrate 6.3g, of which sugars 5.2g; Fat 18.7g, of which saturates 7.1g; Cholesterol 0mg; Calcium 246mg; Fibre 7.6g; Sodium 15mg.

NOODLES AND VEGETABLES IN COCONUT SAUCE

When everyday vegetables are livened up with Thai spices and flavours, the result is a delectable dish that everyone will enjoy. Noodles add bulk and a welcome contrast in texture, and the red curry and coconut sauce marries everything together perfectly.

SERVES FOUR TO SIX

INGREDIENTS
- 30ml/2 tbsp sunflower oil
- 1 lemon grass stalk, finely chopped
- 15ml/1 tbsp Thai red curry paste
- 1 onion, thickly sliced
- 3 courgettes (zucchini), thickly sliced
- 115g/4oz Savoy cabbage, thickly sliced
- 2 carrots, thickly sliced
- 150g/5oz broccoli, stem thickly sliced and head separated into florets
- 2 × 400ml/14fl oz cans coconut milk
- 475ml/16fl oz/2 cups vegetable stock
- 150g/5oz dried egg noodles
- 30ml/2 tbsp soy sauce
- 60ml/4 tbsp chopped fresh coriander (cilantro)

For the garnish
- 2 lemon grass stalks
- 1 bunch fresh coriander (cilantro)
- 8–10 small fresh red chillies

1 Heat the oil in a wok. Add the lemon grass and red curry paste and stir-fry for 2–3 seconds. Add the onion and cook over medium heat, stirring occasionally, until the onion has softened but not browned.

2 Add the courgettes, cabbage, carrots and slices of broccoli stem. Using two spoons, toss the vegetables with the onion mixture. Reduce the heat to low and cook gently, stirring occasionally, for a further 5 minutes.

3 Increase the heat to medium, stir in the coconut milk and vegetable stock and bring to the boil. Add the broccoli florets and the noodles, lower the heat and simmer gently for 20 minutes.

4 Meanwhile, make the garnish. Split the lemon grass stalks lengthways through the root. Gather the coriander into a small bouquet and lay it on a platter, following the curve of the rim.

5 Tuck the lemon grass halves into the coriander bouquet and add the chillies to resemble flowers.

6 Stir the soy sauce and chopped coriander into the noodle mixture. Spoon on to the platter, taking care not to disturb the herb bouquet, and serve immediately.

Energy 192Kcal/808kJ; Protein 5.6g; Carbohydrate 29.4g, of which sugars 11.5g; Fat 6.6g, of which saturates 1.4g; Cholesterol 8mg; Calcium 83mg; Fibre 2.4g; Sodium 554mg.

THAI NOODLES <u>WITH</u> CHINESE CHIVES

THIS RECIPE REQUIRES A LITTLE TIME FOR PREPARATION, BUT THE COOKING TIME IS VERY FAST. EVERYTHING IS COOKED IN A HOT WOK AND SHOULD BE EATEN IMMEDIATELY. THIS IS A FILLING AND TASTY VEGETARIAN DISH, IDEAL FOR A WEEKEND LUNCH.

SERVES FOUR

INGREDIENTS
    350g/12oz dried rice noodles
    1cm/½ in piece fresh root ginger,
      peeled and grated
    30ml/2 tbsp light soy sauce
    45ml/3 tbsp vegetable oil
    225g/8oz Quorn (mycoprotein), cut
      into small cubes
    2 garlic cloves, crushed
    1 large onion, cut into thin wedges
    115g/4oz fried tofu, thinly sliced
    1 fresh green chilli, seeded and
      thinly sliced
    175g/6oz/3 cups beansprouts
    2 large bunches garlic chives, total
      weight about 115g/4oz, cut into
      5cm/2in lengths
    50g/2oz/½ cup roasted
      peanuts, ground
    30ml/2 tbsp dark soy sauce
    30ml/2 tbsp chopped fresh coriander
      (cilantro), and 1 lemon, cut into
      wedges, to garnish

1 Place the noodles in a bowl, cover with warm water and leave to soak for 30 minutes. Drain and set aside.

2 Mix the ginger, light soy sauce and 15ml/1 tbsp of the oil in a bowl. Add the Quorn, then set aside for 10 minutes. Drain, reserving the marinade.

3 Heat 15ml/1 tbsp of the remaining oil in a wok and cook the garlic for a few seconds. Add the Quorn and stir-fry for 3–4 minutes. Using a slotted spoon, transfer to a plate and set aside.

4 Heat the remaining oil in the wok and stir-fry the onion for 3–4 minutes, until softened and tinged with brown. Add the tofu and chilli, stir-fry briefly and then add the noodles. Stir-fry over a medium heat for 4–5 minutes.

5 Stir in the beansprouts, garlic chives and most of the ground peanuts, reserving a little for the garnish. Stir well, then add the Quorn, the dark soy sauce and the reserved marinade.

6 When hot, spoon on to serving plates and garnish with the remaining ground peanuts, the coriander and lemon.

Energy 584Kcal/2435kJ; Protein 19.7g; Carbohydrate 82.9g, of which sugars 7.5g; Fat 18.2g, of which saturates 2.6g; Cholesterol 0mg; Calcium 242mg; Fibre 5.8g; Sodium 984mg.

MEE KROB

THE NAME OF THIS DISH MEANS "DEEP-FRIED NOODLES" AND IT IS VERY POPULAR IN THAILAND. THE TASTE IS A STUNNING COMBINATION OF SWEET AND HOT, SALTY AND SOUR, WHILE THE TEXTURE CONTRIVES TO BE BOTH CRISP AND CHEWY. TO SOME WESTERN PALATES, IT MAY SEEM RATHER UNUSUAL, BUT THIS DELICIOUS DISH IS WELL WORTH MAKING.

SERVES TWO

INGREDIENTS

- vegetable oil, for deep-frying
- 130g/4½oz rice vermicelli noodles

For the sauce
- 30ml/2 tbsp vegetable oil
- 130g/4½oz fried tofu, cut into thin strips
- 2 garlic cloves, finely chopped
- 2 small shallots, finely chopped
- 15ml/1 tbsp light soy sauce
- 30ml/2 tbsp palm sugar (jaggery) or light muscovado (brown) sugar
- 60ml/4 tbsp vegetable stock
- juice of 1 lime
- 2.5ml/½ tsp dried chilli flakes

For the garnish
- 15ml/1 tbsp vegetable oil
- 1 egg, lightly beaten with 15ml/1 tbsp cold water
- 25g/1oz/⅓ cup beansprouts
- 1 spring onion (scallion), thinly shredded
- 1 fresh red chilli, seeded and finely chopped
- 1 whole head pickled garlic, sliced across the bulb so each slice looks like a flower

1 Heat the oil for deep-frying in a wok or large pan to 190°C/375°F or until a cube of bread, added to the oil, browns in about 40 seconds. Add the noodles and deep-fry until golden and crisp. Drain on kitchen paper and set aside.

2 Make the sauce. Heat the oil in a wok, add the fried tofu and cook over a medium heat until crisp. Using a slotted spoon, transfer it to a plate.

3 Add the garlic and shallots to the wok and cook until golden brown. Stir in the soy sauce, sugar, stock, lime juice and chilli flakes. Cook, stirring, until the mixture begins to caramelize.

4 Add the reserved tofu and stir until it has soaked up some of the liquid. Remove the wok from the heat and set aside.

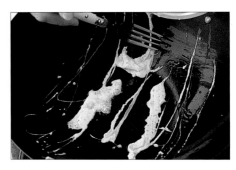

5 Prepare the egg garnish. Heat the oil in a wok or frying pan. Pour in the egg in a thin stream to form trails. As soon as it sets, lift it out with a fish slice or metal spatula and place on a plate.

6 Crumble the noodles into the tofu sauce, mix well, then spoon into warmed serving bowls. Sprinkle with the beansprouts, spring onion, fried egg strips, chilli and pickled garlic "flowers" and serve immediately.

COOK'S TIP

Successful deep-frying depends, to a large extent, on the type of oil used and the temperature to which it is heated. A bland-tasting oil, such as sunflower, will not alter the flavour of the food. All fats have a "smoke point" – the temperature at which they begin to decompose. Most vegetable oils have a high smoke point, with groundnut (peanut) oil the highest of all and so also the safest.

Energy 497Kcal/2075kJ; Protein 10.2g; Carbohydrate 70.2g, of which sugars 18.3g; Fat 19.95g, of which saturates 2.8g; Cholesterol 104.5mg; Calcium 51mg; Fibre .7g; Sodium 583.5mg.

SWEET AND HOT VEGETABLE NOODLES

This noodle dish has the colour of fire, but only the mildest suggestion of heat. Ginger and plum sauce give it its fruity flavour, while lime juice and tamarind paste add a delicious tang to the aromatic stir-fried vegetables and chopped coriander.

SERVES FOUR

INGREDIENTS

130g/4½oz dried rice noodles
30ml/2 tbsp groundnut (peanut) oil
2.5cm/1in piece fresh root ginger,
  sliced into thin batons
1 garlic clove, crushed
130g/4½oz drained canned bamboo
  shoots, sliced into thin batons
2 medium carrots, sliced into batons
130g/4½oz/1½ cups beansprouts
1 small white cabbage, shredded
10ml/2 tsp tamarind paste
30ml/2 tbsp soy sauce
30ml/2 tbsp plum sauce
10ml/2 tsp sesame oil
15ml/1 tbsp palm sugar (jaggery) or
  light muscovado (brown) sugar
juice of ½ lime
90g/3½oz mooli (daikon), sliced into
  thin batons
small bunch fresh coriander
  (cilantro), chopped
60ml/4 tbsp sesame seeds, toasted

1 Cook the noodles in a large pan of boiling water, following the instructions on the packet. Meanwhile, heat the oil in a wok or large frying pan and stir-fry the ginger and garlic for 2–3 minutes over a medium heat, until golden. Drain the noodles and set them aside.

2 Add the bamboo shoots to the wok, increase the heat to high and stir-fry for 5 minutes. Add the carrots, beansprouts and cabbage and stir-fry for a further 5 minutes, until they are beginning to char on the edges.

3 Stir in the tamarind paste, soy and plum sauces, sesame oil, sugar and lime juice. Add the mooli and coriander, toss to mix, then spoon into a warmed bowl, sprinkle with toasted sesame seeds and serve immediately.

COOK'S TIP
Use a large, sharp knife for shredding cabbage. Remove any tough outer leaves, if necessary, then cut the cabbage into quarters. Cut off and discard the hard core from each quarter, place flat side down, then shred the cabbage thinly.

Energy 321Kcal/1333kJ; Protein 7.1g; Carbohydrate 37.8g, of which sugars 9.8g; Fat 15.4g, of which saturates 2.1g; Cholesterol 0mg; Calcium 142mg; Fibre 4.3g; Sodium 413mg.

VEGETABLE NOODLES WITH BEAN SAUCE

YELLOW BEAN SAUCE ADDS A DISTINCTIVE CHINESE FLAVOUR TO THIS WONDERFULLY SIMPLE DISH OF SPICY VEGETABLES AND NOODLES. THE SAUCE IS MADE FROM FERMENTED YELLOW BEANS AND HAS A MARVELLOUS TEXTURE AND SPICY, AROMATIC FLAVOUR, IF USED IN THE RIGHT PROPORTION.

SERVES FOUR

INGREDIENTS
- 150g/5oz thin egg noodles
- 200g/7oz baby leeks, sliced lengthways
- 200g/7oz baby courgettes (zucchini), halved lengthways
- 200g/7oz sugarsnap peas, trimmed
- 200g/7oz peas
- 15ml/1 tbsp sunflower oil
- 5 garlic cloves, sliced
- 45ml/3 tbsp yellow bean sauce
- 45ml/3 tbsp sweet chilli sauce
- 30ml/2 tbsp sweet soy sauce
- roasted cashew nuts, to garnish

1 Cook the noodles according to the packet instructions, drain and set aside.

2 Line a large bamboo steamer with perforated baking parchment and place the leeks, courgettes and both types of peas in it.

3 Cover the steamer and suspend it over a wok of simmering water. Steam the vegetables for about 5 minutes, then remove and set aside.

4 Pour the water from the wok and wipe dry with kitchen paper. Pour the sunflower oil into the wok and place over a medium heat. Add the sliced garlic and stir-fry for 1–2 minutes.

5 In a separate bowl, mix together the yellow bean, sweet chilli and soy sauces, then pour into the wok. Stir to mix with the garlic, then add the steamed vegetables and the noodles and toss together to combine.

6 Cook the vegetables and noodles for 2–3 minutes, stirring frequently, until heated through.

7 To serve, divide the noodles among four warmed serving bowls and scatter over the cashew nuts to garnish.

Energy 296Kcal/1241kJ; Protein 14.2g; Carbohydrate 44.9g, of which sugars 7.4g; Fat 7.8g, of which saturates 1.6g; Cholesterol 11mg; Calcium 61mg; Fibre 8.2g; Sodium 209mg.

CANTONESE FRIED NOODLES

CHOW MEIN IS HUGELY POPULAR WITH THE THRIFTY CHINESE, WHO BELIEVE IN TURNING LEFTOVERS INTO TASTY DISHES. FOR THIS DELICIOUS DISH, BOILED NOODLES ARE FRIED TO FORM A CRISPY CRUST, WHICH IS TOPPED WITH A SAVOURY SAUCE CONTAINING WHATEVER TASTES GOOD AND NEEDS EATING UP.

SERVES TWO TO THREE

INGREDIENTS
225g/8oz can bamboo shoots, drained
1 leek, trimmed
150g/5oz Chinese leaves (Chinese cabbage)
25g/1oz Chinese dried mushrooms, soaked for 30 minutes in 120ml/ 4fl oz/½ cup warm water
450g/1lb cooked egg noodles (225g/8oz dried), drained well
90ml/6 tbsp vegetable oil
30ml/2 tbsp dark soy sauce
15ml/1 tbsp cornflour (cornstarch)
15ml/1 tbsp rice wine or sherry
5ml/1 tsp sesame oil
5ml/1 tsp sugar
salt and ground black pepper

1 Slice the bamboo shoots and leek into matchsticks. Cut the Chinese leaves into 2.5cm/1in diamond-shaped pieces and sprinkle with salt.

2 Drain the mushrooms, reserving 90ml/6 tbsp of the soaking water. Cut off and discard the stems, then slice the caps finely. Pat the noodles dry with kitchen paper. Divide into three piles.

3 Heat a third of the oil in a large wok or frying pan and sauté one pile of noodles. After turning it over once, press the noodles evenly against the bottom of the pan with a wooden spatula until they form a flat, even cake. Cook over medium heat for about 4 minutes or until the noodles at the bottom have become crisp.

4 Turn the noodle cake over with a spatula or fish slice or invert on to a large plate and slide back into the wok. Cook for 3 minutes more, then slide on to a heated plate. Keep warm. Repeat with the other two piles of noodles.

5 Heat 30ml/2 tbsp of the remaining oil in the wok. Add the strips of leek, and stir-fry for 10–15 seconds. Sprinkle over half of the the soy sauce and then add the bamboo shoots and the mushrooms, with salt and pepper to taste. Toss over the heat for 1 minute, then transfer this mixture to a plate and set aside.

6 Heat the remaining oil in the wok and sauté the Chinese leaves for 1 minute. Return the vegetable mixture to the wok and sauté with the leaves for 30 seconds, stirring constantly.

7 Mix the cornflour with the reserved mushroom water. Stir into the wok along with the rice wine or sherry, sesame oil, sugar and remaining soy sauce. Cook for 15 seconds to thicken. Divide the noodles among 2–3 serving dishes and pile the vegetables on top.

Energy 481Kcal/2006kJ; Protein 24.4g; Carbohydrate 28.9g, of which sugars 7.8g; Fat 30.5g, of which saturates 5.7g; Cholesterol 53mg; Calcium 67mg; Fibre 4.4g; Sodium 791mg.

SICHUAN NOODLES <u>WITH</u> SESAME SAUCE

NOODLES AND ASIAN VEGETABLES SEEM MADE FOR EACH OTHER, AND WHEN THE MARRIAGE TAKES PLACE IN A WOK, WITH A FINE SAUCE TO GUARANTEE HARMONY, THE RESULTS ARE INEVITABLY EXCELLENT. ROASTED NUTS ADD TEXTURE WHILE BOOSTING THE NUTRITIONAL VALUE OF THIS DISH.

SERVES THREE TO FOUR

INGREDIENTS

- 450g/1lb fresh or 225g/8oz dried egg noodles
- 1/2 cucumber, sliced lengthways, seeded and diced
- 4–6 spring onions (scallions)
- a bunch of radishes, about 115g/4oz
- 225g/8oz mooli (daikon), peeled
- 115g/4oz/2 cups beansprouts, rinsed then left in iced water and drained
- 60ml/4 tbsp groundnut (peanut) oil or sunflower oil
- 2 garlic cloves, crushed
- 45ml/3 tbsp toasted sesame paste
- 15ml/1 tbsp sesame oil
- 15ml/1 tbsp light soy sauce
- 5–10ml/1–2 tsp chilli sauce, to taste
- 15ml/1 tbsp rice vinegar
- 120ml/4fl oz/1/2 cup vegetable stock or water
- 5ml/1 tsp sugar, or to taste
- salt and ground black pepper
- roasted peanuts or cashew nuts, to garnish

1 If using fresh noodles, cook them in boiling water for 1 minute then drain well. Rinse the noodles in fresh water and drain again. Cook dried noodles according to the instructions on the packet, draining and rinsing them as for fresh noodles.

2 Sprinkle the cucumber with salt, leave for 15 minutes, rinse well, then drain and pat dry on kitchen paper. Place in a large salad bowl.

3 Cut the spring onions into fine shreds. Cut the radishes in half and slice finely. Coarsely grate the mooli using a mandolin or a food processor. Add all the vegetables to the cucumber and toss gently.

4 Heat half the oil in a wok or frying pan and stir-fry the noodles for about 1 minute. Using a slotted spoon, transfer the noodles to a large serving bowl and keep warm. Add the remaining oil to the wok. When it is hot, fry the garlic to flavour the oil.

COOK'S TIP
When warming through the sauce, it is important not to heat it too much or too quickly to avoid it over-thickening.

5 Remove from the heat and stir in the sesame paste, with the sesame oil, soy and chilli sauces, vinegar and stock or water. Add a little sugar and season to taste. Warm through over a gentle heat. Pour the sauce over the noodles and toss well. Garnish with the nuts and serve with the vegetables.

Energy 440Kcal/1838kJ; Protein 11g; Carbohydrate 44.6g, of which sugars 4.6g; Fat 25.4g, of which saturates 4.1g; Cholesterol 17mg; Calcium 128mg; Fibre 4.2g; Sodium 384mg.

INDIAN MEE GORENG

THIS IS A TRULY INTERNATIONAL DISH, COMBINING INDIAN, CHINESE AND WESTERN INGREDIENTS. IT IS A DELICIOUS TREAT FOR LUNCH OR SUPPER AND IN SINGAPORE AND MALAYSIA CAN BE BOUGHT IN MANY STREETS FROM ONE OF THE MANY FOODSELLERS' STALLS.

2 If using fried tofu, cut each cube in half, refresh it in a pan of boiling water, then drain well. Heat 30ml/2 tbsp of the oil in a large frying pan. If using plain tofu, cut into cubes and fry until brown, then lift it out with a slotted spoon and set aside.

3 Beat the eggs with the water. Add to the oil in the frying pan and cook without stirring until set. Flip over, cook the other side, then slide it out of the pan, roll up and slice thinly.

4 Heat the remaining oil in a wok and fry the onion and garlic for 2–3 minutes. Add the drained noodles, soy sauce, ketchup and chilli sauce. Toss well over medium heat for 2 minutes.

SERVES FOUR TO SIX

INGREDIENTS
- 450g/1lb fresh yellow egg noodles
- 60–90ml/4–6 tbsp vegetable oil
- 115g/4oz fried tofu or 150g/5oz firm tofu
- 2 eggs
- 30ml/2 tbsp water
- 1 onion, sliced
- 1 garlic clove, crushed
- 15ml/1 tbsp light soy sauce
- 30–45ml/2–3 tbsp tomato ketchup
- 15ml/1 tbsp chilli sauce (or to taste)
- 1 large cooked potato, diced
- 4 spring onions (scallions), cut in half and shredded
- 1–2 fresh green chillies

1 Bring a large pan of water to the boil, add the fresh egg noodles and cook for just 2 minutes. Drain the noodles and immediately rinse them under cold water to halt cooking. Drain again and set aside, spreading them out on a large platter to dry.

5 Add the diced potato to the wok. Seed and finely slice the green chilli Reserve a few shredded spring onions for the garnish and stir the rest into the noodles with the chilli and tofu.

6 When hot, stir in the omelette. Serve on a hot platter garnished with the remaining spring onion.

Energy 478Kcal/2010kJ; Protein 16.8g; Carbohydrate 64.2g, of which sugars 5.1g; Fat 18.9g, of which saturates 3.2g; Cholesterol 86mg; Calcium 323mg; Fibre 2.9g; Sodium 466mg.

SWEET AND SOUR VEGETABLES WITH TOFU

BIG, BOLD AND BEAUTIFUL, THIS IS A HEARTY STIR-FRY THAT WILL SATISFY THE HUNGRIEST GUESTS. STIR-FRIES ARE ALWAYS A GOOD CHOICE WHEN ENTERTAINING, BECAUSE YOU CAN PREPARE THE INGREDIENTS AHEAD OF TIME AND THEN COOK THEM INCREDIBLY QUICKLY IN THE WOK.

SERVES FOUR

INGREDIENTS
- 4 shallots
- 3 garlic cloves
- 30ml/2 tbsp groundnut (peanut) oil
- 250g/9oz Chinese leaves (Chinese cabbage), shredded
- 8 baby corn cobs, sliced on the diagonal
- 2 red (bell) peppers, seeded and thinly sliced
- 200g/7oz/1¾ cups mangetouts (snow peas), trimmed and sliced
- 250g/9oz tofu, rinsed, drained and cut in 1cm/½ in cubes
- 60ml/4 tbsp vegetable stock
- 30ml/2 tbsp light soy sauce
- 15ml/1 tbsp granulated sugar
- 30ml/2 tbsp rice vinegar
- 2.5ml/½ tsp dried chilli flakes
- small bunch coriander (cilantro), chopped

1 Slice the shallots thinly using a sharp knife. Finely chop the garlic.

2 Heat the oil in a wok or large frying pan and cook the shallots and garlic for 2–3 minutes over a medium heat, until golden. Do not let the garlic burn or it will taste bitter.

3 Add the shredded cabbage, toss over the heat for 30 seconds, then add the corn cobs and repeat the process.

4 Add the red peppers, mangetouts and tofu in the same way, each time adding a single ingredient and tossing it over the heat for about 30 seconds before adding the next ingredient.

5 Pour in the stock and soy sauce. Mix together the sugar and vinegar in a small bowl, stirring until the sugar has dissolved, then add to the wok or pan. Sprinkle over the chilli flakes and coriander, toss to mix well and serve.

Energy 180Kcal/751kJ; Protein 9.1g; Carbohydrate 17g, of which sugars 15.6g; Fat 8.7g, of which saturates 1.1g; Cholesterol 0mg; Calcium 386mg; Fibre 4.1g; Sodium 575mg.

SAVOURY FRIED RICE

THE TITLE MAKES THIS SOUND LIKE RATHER AN ORDINARY DISH, BUT IT IS NOTHING OF THE KIND.
CHILLI, NUTS AND TOASTED COCONUT GIVE THE MIXTURE OF RICE AND BEANS AND WILTED GREENS
PLENTY OF FLAVOUR, AND THE EGG THAT IS STIRRED IN PROVIDES THE PROTEIN CONTENT.

SERVES TWO

INGREDIENTS
   30ml/2 tbsp vegetable oil
   2 garlic cloves, finely chopped
   1 small fresh red chilli, seeded and
     finely chopped
   50g/2oz/½ cup cashew nuts, toasted
   50g/2oz/⅔ cup desiccated
     (dry unsweetened shredded)
     coconut, toasted
   2.5ml/½ tsp palm sugar (jaggery) or
     light muscovado (brown) sugar
   30ml/2 tbsp light soy sauce
   15ml/1 tbsp rice vinegar
   1 egg
   115g/4oz/1 cup green beans, sliced
   ½ spring cabbage or 115g/4oz spring
     greens (collards) or pak choi (bok
     choy), shredded
   90g/3½oz jasmine rice, cooked
   lime wedges, to serve

1 Heat the oil in a wok or large, heavy frying pan. Add the garlic and cook over a medium to high heat until golden. Do not let it burn or it will taste bitter.

2 Add the red chilli, cashew nuts and toasted coconut to the wok or pan and stir-fry briefly, taking care to prevent the coconut from scorching. Stir in the sugar, soy sauce and rice vinegar. Toss over the heat for 1–2 minutes.

3 Push the stir-fry to one side of the wok or pan and break the egg into the empty side. When the egg is almost set, stir it into the garlic and chilli mixture with a wooden spatula or spoon.

4 Add the green beans, greens and cooked rice. Stir over the heat until the greens have just wilted, then spoon into a dish to serve. Offer the lime wedges separately, for squeezing over the rice.

Energy 570Kcal/2366kJ; Protein 16.1g; Carbohydrate 30.5g, of which sugars 8.7g; Fat 43.6g, of which saturates 18.2g; Cholesterol 95mg; Calcium 187mg; Fibre 8.5g; Sodium 1196mg.

RICE CONGEE

ORIGINATING IN CHINA, THIS DISH HAS NOW SPREAD THROUGHOUT THE WHOLE OF SOUTH-EAST ASIA AND IS LOVED FOR ITS COMFORTING BLANDNESS. IT IS INVARIABLY TEAMED WITH A FEW STRONGLY FLAVOURED ACCOMPANIMENTS TO PROVIDE CONTRASTING TASTES AND TEXTURES.

SERVES TWO

INGREDIENTS
   900ml/1½ pints/3¾ cups
      vegetable stock
   200g/7oz cooked rice
   15ml/1 tbsp Thai fish sauce, or
      mushroom ketchup
   2 heads pickled garlic,
      finely chopped (see Cook's Tip)
   1 celery stick, finely diced
   salt and ground black pepper
To garnish
   30ml/2 tbsp groundnut (peanut) oil
   4 garlic cloves, thinly sliced
   4 small red shallots, finely sliced

1 Make the garnishes by heating the groundnut oil in a wok and cooking the garlic and shallots over a low heat until brown. Drain on kitchen paper and reserve for the soup.

2 Pour the stock into a large pan. Bring to the boil and add the rice.

4 Stir in the sauce and pickled garlic and simmer for 10 minutes to let the flavours develop. Stir in the celery.

5 Serve the rice congee in individual warmed bowls. Sprinkle the prepared garlic and shallots on top and season with plenty of ground pepper.

COOK'S TIP
Pickled garlic has a distinctive flavour and is available from Asian food stores.

Energy 509Kcal/2126kJ; Protein 27.3g; Carbohydrate 37.2g, of which sugars 0.8g; Fat 29g, of which saturates 6.3g; Cholesterol 74mg; Calcium 39mg; Fibre 1.8g; Sodium 86mg.

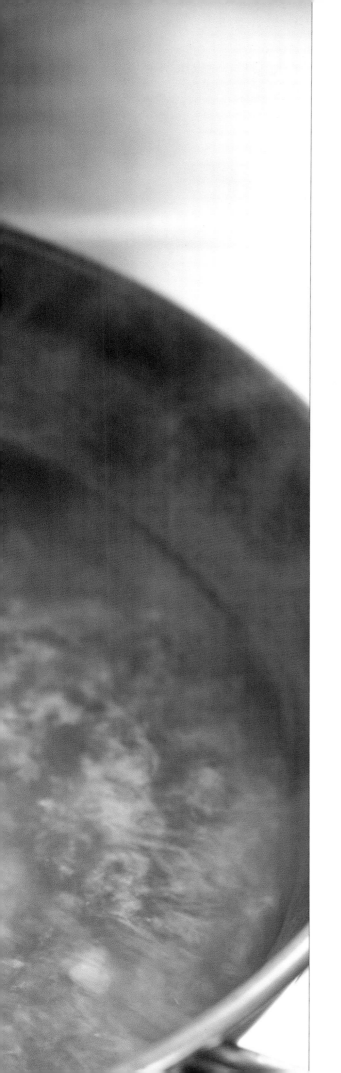

SALADS AND SIDE DISHES

Although it is perfectly possible to cook an entire meal in a

wok — and many of the recipes in this book let you do just

that — it can also be a very useful utensil for making side

dishes. A vegetable stir-fry may not be the first dish that

comes to mind for serving with the Sunday roast, but why

not? The crisp, clean flavours would be an ideal contrast to

more classic accompaniments, and the colours would look

lovely on the plate. A wok is great for making a warm

salad, too, whether you simply use it for dry-roasting rice,

as in Bamboo Shoot Salad, or let it take a leading role in a

dish such as Spicy Chickpeas with Spinach.

BAMBOO SHOOT SALAD

GRAINS OF GLUTINOUS RICE THAT HAVE BEEN DRY-ROASTED IN THE WOK, THEN GROUND TO FINE CRUMBS, MAKE AN INTERESTING ADDITION TO THIS COLOURFUL AND UNUSUAL SALAD. THE CRUNCH THEY PROVIDE MAKES A GOOD CONTRAST TO THE SILKY SMOOTHNESS OF THE BAMBOO SHOOTS.

SERVES FOUR

INGREDIENTS

400g/14oz canned bamboo shoots, in large pieces
25g/1oz/about 3 tbsp Thai sticky rice, cooked
30ml/2 tbsp chopped shallots
15ml/1 tbsp chopped garlic
45ml/3 tbsp chopped spring onions (scallions)
30ml/2 tbsp Thai fish sauce
30ml/2 tbsp fresh lime juice
5ml/1 tsp granulated sugar
2.5ml/½ tsp dried chilli flakes
20–25 small fresh mint leaves
15ml/1 tbsp toasted sesame seeds

1 Rinse the bamboo shoots under cold running water, then drain them and pat them thoroughly dry with kitchen paper and set them aside.

2 Dry-roast the rice in a wok until it is golden brown. Leave to cool slightly, then grind to find crumbs in a mortar.

3 Transfer the rice to a bowl and add the shallots, garlic, spring onions, fish sauce, lime juice, sugar, chilli flakes and half the mint leaves. Mix well.

4 Add the bamboo shoots to the bowl and toss to mix. Serve sprinkled with the toasted sesame seeds and mint.

Energy 85Kcal/357kJ; Protein 4.2g; Carbohydrate 11.3g, of which sugars 4.1g; Fat 2.7g, of which saturates 0.4g; Cholesterol 0mg; Calcium 51mg; Fibre 2g; Sodium 6mg.

NOODLE, TOFU AND SPROUTED BEAN SALAD

BEAN THREAD NOODLES LOOK LIKE SPUN GLASS ON THIS STUNNING SALAD, WHICH OWES ITS GOODNESS TO FRESH BEANSPROUTS, DICED TOMATO AND CUCUMBER IN A SWEET-SOUR DRESSING. THE SALAD TAKES ONLY MINUTES TO TOSS TOGETHER.

SERVES FOUR

INGREDIENTS

25g/1oz bean thread noodles
500g/1¼lb mixed sprouted beans
   and pulses (aduki, chickpea, mung,
   red lentil)
4 spring onions (scallions),
   finely shredded
115g/4oz firm tofu, diced
1 ripe plum tomato, seeded
   and diced
½ cucumber, peeled, seeded
   and diced
60ml/4 tbsp chopped fresh
   coriander (cilantro)
45ml/3 tbsp chopped fresh mint
60ml/4 tbsp rice vinegar
10ml/2 tsp caster (superfine) sugar
10ml/2 tsp sesame oil
5ml/1 tsp chilli oil
salt and ground black pepper

1 Place the bean thread noodles in a bowl and pour over enough boiling water to cover. Leave to soak for 12–15 minutes.

2 Drain the noodles and then refresh them under cold, running water and drain again. Using a pair of scissors, cut the noodles into roughly 7.5cm/3in lengths and transfer to a bowl.

3 Fill a wok one-third full of boiling water and place over high heat. Add the sprouted beans and pulses and blanch for 1 minute. Drain, transfer to the noodle bowl and add the spring onions, tofu, tomato, cucumber and herbs.

4 Combine the rice vinegar, sugar, sesame oil and chilli oil and toss into the noodle mixture. Transfer to a serving dish and chill for 30 minutes before serving.

COOK'S TIP
If you leave the salad to stand for half an hour to an hour, the flavours will improve as they develop and fuse together.

Energy 113Kcal/475kJ; Protein 6.8g; Carbohydrate 14.1g, of which sugars 6.6g; Fat 3.5g, of which saturates 0.5g; Cholesterol 0mg; Calcium 184mg; Fibre 2.4g; Sodium 11mg.

FRAGRANT MUSHROOMS IN LETTUCE LEAVES

THIS QUICK AND EASY VEGETABLE DISH IS SERVED ON LETTUCE LEAF "SAUCERS" SO CAN BE EATEN WITH THE FINGERS — A GREAT TREAT FOR CHILDREN AND FUN FOR ADULTS TOO.

SERVES TWO

INGREDIENTS
  30ml/2 tbsp vegetable oil
  2 garlic cloves, finely chopped
  2 baby cos or romaine lettuces,
    or 2 Little Gem (Bibb) lettuces
  1 lemon grass stalk, finely chopped
  2 kaffir lime leaves, rolled in
    cylinders and thinly sliced
  200g/7oz/3 cups oyster or chestnut
    mushrooms, sliced
  1 small fresh red chilli, seeded
    and finely chopped
  juice of ½ lemon
  30ml/2 tbsp light soy sauce
  5ml/1 tsp palm sugar (jaggery) or
    light muscovado (brown) sugar
  small bunch fresh mint leaves

1 Heat the oil in a wok or frying pan. Add the garlic and cook over a medium heat, stirring occasionally, until golden. Do not let it burn or it will taste bitter.

2 Meanwhile, separate the individual lettuce leaves. Wash and dry them, then set them aside in a bowl.

3 Increase the heat under the wok or pan and add the lemon grass, lime leaves and sliced mushrooms. Stir-fry for about 2 minutes.

4 Add the chilli, lemon juice, soy sauce and sugar to the wok or pan. Toss the mixture over the heat to combine the ingredients together, then stir-fry for a further 2 minutes.

5 Arrange the lettuce on a plate. Spoon a small amount of mushroom mixture on to each leaf and top with a mint leaf.

Energy 154Kcal/641kJ; Protein 3.9g; Carbohydrate 7.1g, of which sugars 6.8g; Fat 12.5g, of which saturates 1.6g; Cholesterol 0mg; Calcium 66mg; Fibre 2.9g; Sodium 1079mg.

CABBAGE SALAD

THIS IS A SIMPLE AND DELICIOUS WAY OF SERVING A SOMEWHAT MUNDANE VEGETABLE. THE WOK COMES IN HANDY FOR STIR-FRYING THE AROMATIC VEGETABLES THAT FLAVOUR THE CABBAGE.

SERVES FOUR TO SIX

INGREDIENTS
30ml/2 tbsp vegetable oil
2 large fresh red chillies, seeded and
cut into thin strips
6 garlic cloves, thinly sliced
6 shallots, thinly sliced
1 small cabbage, shredded
30ml/2 tbsp coarsely chopped
roasted peanuts, to garnish
For the dressing
30ml/2 tbsp Thai fish sauce
grated rind of 1 lime
30ml/2 tbsp fresh lime juice
120ml/4fl oz/½ cup coconut milk

VARIATION
Other vegetables, such as cauliflower, broccoli and Chinese leaves (Chinese cabbage), can be cooked in this way.

1 Make the dressing by mixing the fish sauce, lime rind and juice and coconut milk in a bowl. Whisk until thoroughly combined, then set aside.

2 Heat the oil in a wok. Stir-fry the chillies, garlic and shallots over a medium heat for 3–4 minutes, until the shallots are brown and crisp. Remove with a slotted spoon and set aside.

3 Bring a large pan of lightly salted water to the boil. Add the cabbage and blanch for 2–3 minutes. Tip it into a colander, drain well and put into a bowl.

4 Whisk the dressing again, add it to the warm cabbage and toss to mix. Transfer the salad to a serving dish. Sprinkle with the fried shallot mixture and the peanuts. Serve immediately.

Energy 96Kcal/400kJ; Protein 2.7g; Carbohydrate 7.7g, of which sugars 6.6g; Fat 6.2g, of which saturates 0.9g; Cholesterol 0mg; Calcium 50mg; Fibre 2.2g; Sodium 147mg.

LIGHT AND CRISPY SEVEN-SPICE AUBERGINES

THAI SEVEN SPICE POWDER IS A COMMERCIAL BLEND OF SPICES, INCLUDING CORIANDER, CUMIN, CINNAMON, STAR ANISE, CHILLI, CLOVES AND LEMON PEEL. IT GIVES THESE AUBERGINES A LOVELY WARM FLAVOUR THAT GOES VERY WELL WITH THE LIGHT, CURRY BATTER.

SERVES FOUR

INGREDIENTS

    2 egg whites
    90ml/6 tbsp cornflour (cornstarch)
    5ml/1 tsp salt
    15ml/1 tbsp Thai or Chinese seven-
      spice powder
    15ml/1 tbsp mild chilli powder
    500g/1¼lb aubergines (eggplants),
      thinly sliced
    sunflower oil, for deep-frying
    fresh mint leaves, to garnish
    steamed rice or noodles and hot
      chilli sauce, to serve

1 Whisk the egg whites in a large bowl until light and foamy, but not dry.

2 Combine the cornflour, salt, seven-spice powder and chilli powder and spread evenly on to a large plate.

3 Fill a wok one-third full of oil and heat to 180°C/350°F (or until a cube of bread, dropped into the oil, browns in 40 seconds).

4 Dip the aubergine slices in the egg white and then into the spiced flour mixture to coat. Deep-fry in batches for 3–4 minutes, or until crisp and golden. Drain on kitchen paper and keep warm.

5 Serve the aubergine garnished with mint leaves and with hot chilli sauce on the side for dipping.

Energy 203Kcal/850kJ; Protein 2.7g; Carbohydrate 23.5g, of which sugars 2.5g; Fat 11.7g, of which saturates 1.4g; Cholesterol 0mg; Calcium 17mg; Fibre 2.5g; Sodium 45mg.

ASIAN-STYLE COURGETTE FRITTERS

THIS IS A TWIST ON JAPANESE TEMPURA, USING INDIAN SPICES AND GRAM FLOUR IN THE BATTER.
ALSO KNOWN AS BESAN, GRAM FLOUR IS MORE COMMONLY USED IN INDIAN COOKING AND GIVES A
WONDERFULLY CRISP TEXTURE, WHILE THE COURGETTE BATON INSIDE BECOMES MELTINGLY TENDER.

SERVES FOUR

INGREDIENTS
   90g/3½oz/¾ cup gram flour
   5ml/1 tsp baking powder
   2.5ml/½ tsp ground turmeric
   10ml/2 tsp ground coriander
   5ml/1 tsp ground cumin
   5ml/1 tsp chilli powder
   250ml/8fl oz/1 cup beer
   600g/1lb 6oz courgettes (zucchini),
     cut into batons
   sunflower oil, for deep-frying
   salt
   steamed basmati rice, natural (plain)
     yogurt and pickles, to serve

1 Sift the gram flour, baking powder, turmeric, coriander, cumin and chilli powder into a large bowl. Stir lightly to mix through.

2 Season the mixture with salt and then gradually add the beer, mixing gently as you pour it in, to make a thick batter – be careful not to overmix.

3 Fill a large wok, one-third full with sunflower oil and heat to 180°C/350°F or until a cube of bread, dropped into the oil, browns in 45 seconds.

4 Working in batches, dip the courgette batons in the spiced batter and then deep-fry for 1–2 minutes, or until crisp and golden. Lift out of the wok using a slotted spoon. Drain on kitchen paper and keep warm. Serve the courgettes immediately with steamed basmati rice, yogurt and pickles.

Energy 241Kcal/999kJ; Protein 7.3g; Carbohydrate 15.3g, of which sugars 4.6g; Fat 15.6g, of which saturates 1.9g; Cholesterol 0mg; Calcium 83mg; Fibre 3.8g; Sodium 15mg.

FRIED VEGETABLES WITH CHILLI SAUCE

A WOK MAKES THE IDEAL PAN FOR FRYING SLICES OF AUBERGINE, BUTTERNUT SQUASH AND COURGETTE BECAUSE THEY BECOME BEAUTIFULLY TENDER AND SUCCULENT. THE BEATEN EGG IN THIS RECIPE GIVES A SATISFYINGLY SUBSTANTIAL BATTER.

<u>SERVES FOUR</u>

INGREDIENTS

3 large (US extra large) eggs
1 aubergine (eggplant), halved lengthways and cut into long, thin slices
½ small butternut squash, peeled, seeded and cut into long, thin slices
2 courgettes (zucchini), trimmed and cut into long, thin slices
105ml/7 tbsp vegetable or sunflower oil
salt and ground black pepper
sweet chilli sauce, to serve

1 Beat the eggs in a large bowl. Season the egg mixture with salt and pepper. Add the slices of aubergine, butternut squash and courgette. Toss the vegetables slices until they are coated all over in the egg.

2 Have a warmed dish ready lined with kitchen paper. Heat the oil in a wok. When it is hot, add the vegetables, one strip at a time, making sure that each strip has plenty of egg clinging to it.

3 Do not cook more than eight strips of vegetable at a time or the oil will cool down too much.

4 As each strip turns golden and is cooked, lift it out, using a wire basket or slotted spoon, and transfer to the plate. Keep hot while cooking the remaining vegetables. Serve with the sweet chilli sauce as a dip.

Energy 281Kcal/1162kJ; Protein 8.8g; Carbohydrate 5.7g, of which sugars 4.8g; Fat 25.1g, of which saturates 3.9g; Cholesterol 171mg; Calcium 92mg; Fibre 3.2g; Sodium 65mg.

INDIAN-STYLE SPICED RED LENTIL DHAL

A KARAHI IS THE INDIAN EQUIVALENT OF THE WOK. HERE IT IS USED TO GREAT EFFECT TO MAKE WHAT CAN ONLY BE DESCRIBED AS CLASSIC COMFORT FOOD. THERE'S NOTHING LIKE A BOWL OF DHAL SPICED WITH MUSTARD SEEDS, CUMIN AND CORIANDER TO CLEAR AWAY THE BLUES.

SERVES FOUR

INGREDIENTS
  30ml/2 tbsp sunflower oil
  1 fresh green chilli, halved
  2 red onions, halved
    and thinly sliced
  10ml/2 tsp crushed garlic
  10ml/2 tsp finely grated fresh
    root ginger
  10ml/2 tsp black mustard seeds
  15ml/1 tbsp cumin seeds
  10ml/2 tsp crushed coriander seeds
  10 curry leaves
  250g/9oz/generous 1 cup red lentils
  2.5ml/½ tsp ground turmeric
  2 plum tomatoes
  salt
  coriander (cilantro) leaves and crispy
    fried onion, to garnish (optional)
  yogurt, poppadums and griddled
    flatbread or naans, to serve

1 Heat a karahi or wok and add the sunflower oil. When it is hot add the green chilli and onions, stir to combine, lower the heat and cook gently for 10–12 minutes, until softened.

2 Increase the heat slightly and add the garlic, ginger, mustard seeds, cumin seeds, coriander seeds and curry leaves and stir-fry for 2–3 minutes.

3 Rinse the lentils in cold water, drain, then add to the wok with 700ml/1 pint 2fl oz/scant 3 cups cold water. Stir in the turmeric and season with salt. Bring to the boil.

4 Chop the tomatoes and add to the wok. Reduce the heat and cook gently for 25–30 minutes, stirring occasionally.

5 Check the seasoning, then garnish with coriander leaves and crispy fried onion, if liked, and serve with yogurt, poppadums and flatbread or naans.

VARIATION
If you prefer, you can use yellow split peas in place of the lentils. Like red lentils, these only need to be rinsed, not soaked, before cooking.

Energy 284Kcal/1198kJ; Protein 16.1g; Carbohydrate 42.7g, of which sugars 7.3g; Fat 6.6g, of which saturates 0.8g; Cholesterol 0mg; Calcium 54mg; Fibre 4.6g; Sodium 29mg.

THAI ASPARAGUS

IF YOU'VE NEVER HAD ASPARAGUS COOKED IN THE WOK, DO YOURSELF A FAVOUR AND TRY THIS DELICIOUS RECIPE. THE ZINGY FLAVOURS OF GALANGAL AND CHILLI, COUPLED WITH THE SWEET AND SPICY SAUCE TRANSFORM WHAT CAN BE A SUBTLE TASTE INTO SOMETHING OF A SENSATION.

SERVES FOUR

INGREDIENTS
350g/12oz asparagus stalks
30ml/2 tbsp vegetable oil
1 garlic clove, crushed
15ml/1 tbsp sesame seeds, toasted
2.5cm/1in piece fresh galangal, finely shredded
1 fresh red chilli, seeded and finely chopped
15ml/1 tbsp Thai fish sauce
15ml/1 tbsp light soy sauce
45ml/3 tbsp water
5ml/1 tsp palm sugar (jaggery) or light muscovado (brown) sugar

VARIATIONS
Try this with broccoli or pak choi (bok choy). The sauce also works very well with green beans.

1 Snap the asparagus stalks. They will break naturally at the junction between the woody base and the more tender portion of the stalk. Discard the woody parts of the stems.

2 Heat a wok and add the oil. Stir-fry the garlic, sesame seeds and galangal for 3–4 seconds, until the garlic is just beginning to turn golden.

3 Add the asparagus stalks and chilli, toss to mix, then add the fish sauce, soy sauce, water and sugar.

4 Using two spoons, toss over the heat for a further 2 minutes, or until the asparagus just begins to soften and the liquid is reduced by half. Serve the asparagus immediately, with the sauce spooned over it.

Energy 99Kcal/410kJ; Protein 3.4g; Carbohydrate 3.1g, of which sugars 3g; Fat 8.2g, of which saturates 1.1g; Cholesterol 0mg; Calcium 50mg; Fibre 1.8g; Sodium 269mg.

BABY ASPARAGUS <u>WITH</u> CRISPY NOODLES

TENDER ASPARAGUS SPEARS TOSSED WITH SESAME SEEDS AND SERVED ON A BED OF CRISPY, DEEP-FRIED NOODLES MAKES A LOVELY DISH FOR CASUAL ENTERTAINING. THE LIGHTLY COOKED ASPARAGUS RETAINS ALL ITS FRESH FLAVOUR AND BITE AND CONTRASTS WONDERFULLY WITH THE NOODLES.

SERVES FOUR

INGREDIENTS
15ml/1 tbsp sunflower oil
350g/12oz thin asparagus spears
5ml/1 tsp salt
5ml/1 tsp ground black pepper
5ml/1 tsp golden caster
  (superfine) sugar
30ml/2 tbsp Chinese cooking wine
45ml/3 tbsp light soy sauce
60ml/4 tbsp oyster sauce
10ml/2 tsp sesame oil
60ml/4 tbsp toasted
  sesame seeds
For the noodles
50g/2oz dried bean thread noodles
  or thin rice noodles
sunflower oil, for deep-frying

1 First make the crispy noodles. Fill a wok one-third full of oil and heat to 180°C/350°F or until a cube of bread, dropped into the oil, browns in 45 seconds. Add a small bunch of noodles to the oil; they will crisp and puff up in seconds.

2 Using a slotted spoon, remove from the wok and drain on kitchen paper. Set aside. Cook the remaining noodles in the same way.

COOK'S TIP
Bean thread noodles, also sold as cellophane or transparent noodles, an be difficult to track down outside big cities, so buy a few packets when you get the chance, as they make excellent store-cupboard standbys.

3 Heat a clean wok over a high heat and add the sunflower oil. Add the asparagus and stir-fry for 3 minutes.

4 Add the salt, pepper, sugar, wine and both sauces to the wok and stir-fry for 2–3 minutes. Add the sesame oil, toss to combine and remove from the heat.

5 To serve, divide the crispy noodles between 4 warmed plates or bowls and top with the asparagus and juices. Scatter over the toasted sesame seeds and serve immediately.

VARIATION
Try this with baby leeks. Toss them in the sauce until just tender.

Energy 210Kcal/872kJ; Protein 3.8g; Carbohydrate 18.2g, of which sugars 7.7g; Fat 13g, of which saturates 1.6g; Cholesterol 0mg; Calcium 30mg; Fibre 1.6g; Sodium 1540mg.

HERB AND CHILLI AUBERGINES

PLUMP AND JUICY AUBERGINES ARE DELICIOUS STEAMED IN THE WOK UNTIL TENDER AND THEN TOSSED IN A FRAGRANT MINTY DRESSING WITH CORIANDER AND CRUNCHY PEANUTS AND WATER CHESTNUTS. THE COMBINATION OF TEXTURES AND FLAVOURS IS ABSOLUTELY SENSATIONAL.

SERVES FOUR

INGREDIENTS

500g/1¼lb firm, baby aubergines (eggplants)
30ml/2 tbsp sunflower oil
6 garlic cloves, very finely chopped
15ml/1 tbsp very finely chopped fresh root ginger
8 spring onions (scallions), cut diagonally into 2.5cm/1in lengths
2 fresh red chillies, seeded and thinly sliced
45ml/3 tbsp light soy sauce
15ml/1 tbsp Chinese rice wine
15ml/1 tbsp caster (superfine) sugar or palm sugar (jaggery)
a handful of fresh mint leaves
30–45ml/2–3 tbsp roughly chopped fresh coriander (cilantro) leaves
115g/4oz water chestnuts
50g/2oz/½ cup roasted peanuts, roughly chopped
steamed egg noodles or rice, to serve

1 Cut the aubergines in half lengthways and place on a heatproof plate.

2 Place a steamer rack in a wok and add 5cm/2in of water. Bring the water to the boil and lower the plate on to the rack and reduce the heat to low.

3 Cover and steam the aubergines for 25–30 minutes, until they are cooked through. (Check the water level regularly, adding more if necessary.) Set the aubergines aside to cool.

4 Place the oil in a clean, dry wok and place over a medium heat. When hot, add the garlic, ginger, spring onions and chillies and stir-fry for 2–3 minutes. Remove from the heat and stir in the soy sauce, rice wine and sugar.

5 Add the mint leaves, chopped coriander, water chestnuts and peanuts to the aubergine and toss. Pour the garlic-ginger mixture evenly over the vegetables, toss gently and serve with steamed egg noodles or rice.

Energy 177Kcal/739kJ; Protein 6.2g; Carbohydrate 12.1g, of which sugars 9g; Fat 12g, of which saturates 1.9g; Cholesterol 0mg; Calcium 46mg; Fibre 4.4g; Sodium 823mg.

STEAMED VEGETABLES WITH CHILLI DIP

AN INEXPENSIVE BAMBOO STEAMER IS A GREAT WOK ACCESSORY, MAKING IT POSSIBLE TO COOK VEGETABLES QUICKLY AND EASILY SO THAT THEY RETAIN MAXIMUM NUTRIENTS AND KEEP THEIR COLOUR. MIX IN FRESH VEGETABLES, ADD A SPICY DIP AND YOU HAVE A HEALTHY AND TASTY DISH.

SERVES FOUR

INGREDIENTS
  1 head broccoli, divided
    into florets
  130g/4½oz/1 cup green
    beans, trimmed
  130g/4½oz asparagus, trimmed
  ½ head cauliflower, divided
    into florets
  8 baby corn cobs
  130g/4½oz mangetouts (snow peas)
    or sugar snap peas
  salt
For the dip
  1 fresh green chilli, seeded
  4 garlic cloves, peeled
  4 shallots, peeled
  2 tomatoes, halved
  5 pea aubergines (eggplants)
  30ml/2 tbsp lemon juice
  30ml/2 tbsp soy sauce
  2.5ml/½ tsp salt
  5ml/1 tsp granulated sugar

COOK'S TIP
Cauliflower varieties with pale green curds have a more delicate flavour than those with white curds. Look out for baby brassicas – miniature cauliflowers and heads of broccoli – for serving whole.

1 Place the broccoli, green beans, asparagus and cauliflower in a bamboo steamer and steam over boiling water in a wok for about 4 minutes, until just tender but still with a "bite". Transfer to a bowl and add the corn cobs and mangetouts or sugar snap peas. Season to taste with a little salt. Toss to mix.

2 Make the dip. Preheat the grill (broiler). Wrap the chilli, garlic cloves, shallots, tomatoes and aubergines in a foil package. Grill (broil) for 10 minutes, until the vegetables have softened, turning the package over once or twice.

3 Unwrap the foil and tip its contents into a mortar or food processor. Add the lemon juice, soy sauce, salt and sugar. Pound with a pestle or process to a fairly liquid paste.

4 Scrape the dip into a serving bowl or four individual bowls. Serve, surrounded by the steamed and raw vegetables.

VARIATIONS
You can use a combination of other vegetables if you like. Use pak choi (bok choy) instead of the cauliflower or substitute raw baby carrots for the corn cobs and mushrooms in place of the mangetouts (snow peas).

Energy 129Kcal/541kJ; Protein 13.3g; Carbohydrate 13.3g, of which sugars 11.3g; Fat 2.8g, of which saturates 0.6g; Cholesterol 0mg; Calcium 138mg; Fibre 8.5g; Sodium 772mg.

STEAMED AUBERGINES <u>WITH</u> SESAME SAUCE

THIS JAPANESE RECIPE REPRESENTS A TYPICAL ZEN TEMPLE COOKING STYLE. FRESH SEASONAL VEGETABLES ARE CHOSEN AND SIMPLY COOKED WITH CARE. THEN A SAUCE MADE OF CAREFULLY BALANCED FLAVOURS IS ADDED. THIS DISH IS ALSO DELICIOUS COLD.

SERVES FOUR

INGREDIENTS

   2 large aubergines (eggplants)
   400ml/14fl oz/1⅔ cups second dashi
     stock made using water and instant
     dashi powder
   25ml/1½ tbsp caster (superfine)
     sugar
   15ml/1 tbsp shoyu
   15ml/1 tbsp sesame seeds, finely
     ground
   15ml/1 tbsp sake
   15ml/1 tbsp cornflour (cornstarch)
   salt
For the accompanying vegetables
   130g/4½oz shimeji mushrooms
   115g/4oz/¾ cup fine green beans
   100ml/3fl oz/scant ½ cup second
     dashi stock, made using water and
     instant dashi powder
   25ml/1½ tbsp caster (superfine)
     sugar
   15ml/1 tbsp sake
   1.5ml/¼ tsp salt
   dash of shoyu

1 Peel the aubergines and cut them in quarters lengthways. Prick all over with a skewer, then plunge into a bowl of salted water for 30 minutes.

2 Drain the aubergine wedges and place them side by side in a bamboo steamer basket. Place the basket on a trivet, on top of a wok containing boiling water. Cover and steam for 20 minutes. Do not let the water touch the bottom of the steamer basket.

3 Mix the dashi stock, sugar, shoyu and 1.5ml/¼ tsp salt together in a large pan. Gently transfer the aubergines to this pan, then cover and cook over a low heat for a further 15 minutes. Take a few tablespoonfuls of stock from the pan and mix with the ground sesame seeds. Add this mixture to the pan.

4 Thoroughly mix the sake with the cornflour, add to the pan with the aubergines and stock and shake the pan gently, but quickly. When the sauce becomes quite thick, remove the pan from the heat.

5 While the aubergines are cooking, prepare and cook the accompanying vegetables. Cut off the hard base part of the mushrooms and separate the large block into smaller chunks with your fingers. Trim the green beans and cut them in half.

6 Mix the stock with the sugar, sake, salt and shoyu in a shallow pan. Add the green beans and mushrooms and cook for 7 minutes until just tender. Serve the aubergines and their sauce in individual bowls with the accompanying vegetables over the top.

Energy 127Kcal/536kJ; Protein 3.3g; Carbohydrate 20.9g, of which sugars 16.8g; Fat 3.1g, of which saturates 0.5g; Cholesterol 0mg; Calcium 60mg; Fibre 4.3g; Sodium 8mg.

SPICY CHICKPEAS WITH SPINACH

THIS RICHLY FLAVOURED DISH MAKES A GREAT ACCOMPANIMENT TO A DRY CURRY, OR WITH A RICE-BASED STIR FRY. IT IS PARTICULARLY GOOD SERVED DRIZZLED WITH A LITTLE PLAIN YOGURT — THE SHARP, CREAMY FLAVOUR COMPLEMENTS THE COMPLEX SPICES PERFECTLY.

SERVES FOUR

INGREDIENTS
   200g/7oz dried chickpeas
   30ml/2 tbsp sunflower oil
   2 onions, halved and thinly sliced
   10ml/2 tsp ground coriander
   10ml/2 tsp ground cumin
   5ml/1 tsp hot chilli powder
   2.5ml/½ tsp ground turmeric
   15ml/1 tbsp medium curry powder
   400g/14oz can chopped tomatoes
   5ml/1 tsp caster (superfine) sugar
   salt and ground black pepper
   30ml/2 tbsp chopped mint leaves
   115g/4oz baby leaf spinach
   steamed rice or bread, to serve

3 Add the tomatoes, sugar and 105ml/7 tbsp water to the wok and bring to the boil. Cover, reduce the heat and simmer gently for 15 minutes.

4 Add the chickpeas to the wok, season well and cook gently for 8–10 minutes. Stir in the chopped mint.

5 Divide the spinach leaves between shallow bowls, top with the chickpea mixture and serve with some steamed rice or bread.

1 Soak the chickpeas in cold water overnight. Drain, rinse and place in a large pan. Cover with water and bring to the boil. Reduce the heat and simmer for 45 minutes, or until just tender. Drain and set aside.

2 Heat the oil in a wok, add the onions and cook over a low heat for 15 minutes, until lightly golden. Add the ground coriander and cumin, chilli powder, turmeric and curry powder and stir-fry for 1–2 minutes.

COOK'S TIP
You can save time and effort by using canned chickpeas. Tip the contents of two 400g/14oz cans of chickpeas into a colander, rinse gently under cold water and drain before adding to the spicy tomato sauce in the wok. Reheat gently before stirring in the mint.

Energy 267Kcal/1122kJ; Protein 13.3g; Carbohydrate 35.5g, of which sugars 10.2g; Fat 9g, of which saturates 1.1g; Cholesterol 0mg; Calcium 170mg; Fibre 8.2g; Sodium 83mg.

CARROT IN SWEET VINEGAR

FOR THIS JAPANESE SIDE DISH CARROT STRIPS ARE MARINATED IN RICE VINEGAR, SHOYU AND MIRIN. IT IS A GOOD ACCOMPANIMENT FOR RICH DISHES SUCH AS FRIED AUBERGINE WITH MISO SAUCE BELOW.

SERVES FOUR

INGREDIENTS
   2 large carrots, peeled
   5ml/1 tsp salt
   30ml/2 tbsp sesame seeds
For the sweet vinegar marinade
   75ml/5 tbsp rice vinegar
   30ml/2 tbsp shoyu (use the pale
      awakuchi soy sauce if available)
   45ml/3 tbsp mirin

COOK'S TIP
This marinade is called *san bai zu*, and is one of the essential basic sauces in Japanese cooking. Dilute the marinade with 15ml/1 tbsp second dashi stock, then add sesame seeds and a few dashes of sesame oil for a very tasty and healthy salad dressing.

1 Cut the carrots into thin matchsticks, 5cm/2in long. Put the carrots and salt into a mixing bowl, and mix well with your hands. After 25 minutes, rinse the wilted carrot in cold water, then drain.

2 In another bowl, mix together the marinade ingredients. Add the carrots, and leave to marinate for 3 hours.

3 Put a wok on a high heat, add the sesame seeds and toss constantly until the seeds start to pop. Remove from the heat and cool.

4 Chop the sesame seeds with a large, sharp knife on a large chopping board. Place the carrots in a bowl, sprinkle with the sesame seeds and serve cold.

FRIED AUBERGINE WITH MISO SAUCE

THIS WELL-FLAVOURED STIR-FRIED AUBERGINE IS COATED IN A RICH MISO SAUCE. MAKE SURE THE OIL IS SMOKING HOT WHEN ADDING THE AUBERGINE PIECES, SO THEY DO NOT ABSORB TOO MUCH OIL.

SERVES FOUR

INGREDIENTS
   2 large aubergines (eggplants)
   1–2 dried red chillies
   45ml/3 tbsp sake
   45ml/3 tbsp mirin
   45ml/3 tbsp caster (superfine) sugar
   30ml/2 tbsp shoyu
   45ml/3 tbsp red miso (use either the
      dark red aka miso or even darker
      hatcho miso)
   90ml/6 tbsp sesame oil
   salt

VARIATION
Sweet (bell) peppers could also be used for this dish instead of the aubergines (eggplants). Take 1 red, 1 yellow and 2 green peppers. Remove the seeds and chop them into 1cm/½in strips, then follow the rest of the recipe.

1 Cut the aubergines into bitesize pieces and place in a large colander, sprinkle with some salt and leave for 30 minutes to remove the bitter juices. Squeeze the aubergine pieces by hand. Remove the seeds from the chillies and chop the chillies into thin rings.

2 Mix the sake, mirin, sugar and shoyu in a cup. In a separate bowl, mix the red miso with 45ml/3 tbsp water to make a loose paste.

3 Heat the oil in a wok and add the chilli. When you see pale smoke rising from the oil, add the aubergine, and stir-fry for about 8 minutes, or until the aubergine pieces are tender. Lower the heat to medium.

4 Add the sake mixture to the pan, and stir for 2–3 minutes. If the sauce starts to burn, lower the heat. Add the miso paste to the pan and cook, stirring, for another 2 minutes. Serve hot.

Energy 66Kcal/272kJ; Protein 1.9g; Carbohydrate 4.6g, of which sugars 4.3g; Fat 4.5g, of which saturates 0.7g; Cholesterol 0mg; Calcium 64mg; Fibre 1.8g; Sodium 1039mg.
Energy 94Kcal/397kJ; Protein 1.8g; Carbohydrate 16.8g, of which sugars 16.4g; Fat 1.4g, of which saturates 0.3g; Cholesterol 0mg; Calcium 24mg; Fibre 3g; Sodium 806mg.

PAK CHOI WITH LIME DRESSING

THE LIME DRESSING FOR THIS THAI SPECIALITY IS TRADITIONALLY MADE USING FISH SAUCE, BUT VEGETARIANS COULD USE MUSHROOM SAUCE INSTEAD. THIS IS A WOK DISH THAT PACKS A FIERY PUNCH; USE FEWER CHILLIES IF YOU PREFER, OR REMOVE THE SEEDS BEFORE STIR-FRYING.

SERVES FOUR

INGREDIENTS
  30ml/2 tbsp oil
  3 fresh red chillies, cut into
    thin strips
  4 garlic cloves, thinly sliced
  6 spring onions (scallions),
    sliced diagonally
  2 pak choi (bok choy), shredded
  15ml/1 tbsp crushed peanuts
For the dressing
  30ml/2 tbsp fresh lime juice
  15–30ml/1–2 tbsp Thai fish sauce
  250ml/8fl oz/1 cup coconut milk

1 Make the dressing. Put the lime juice and fish sauce in a bowl and mix well together, then gradually whisk in the coconut milk until combined.

2 Heat the oil in a wok and stir-fry the chillies for 2–3 minutes, until crisp. Transfer to a plate using a slotted spoon. Add the garlic to the wok and stir-fry for 30–60 seconds, until golden brown. Transfer to the plate.

3 Stir-fry the white parts of the spring onions for about 2–3 minutes, then add the green parts and stir-fry for 1 minute more. Transfer to the plate.

4 Bring a large pan of lightly salted water to the boil and add the pak choi. Stir twice, then drain immediately.

5 Place the pak choi in a large bowl, add the dressing and toss to mix. Spoon into a large serving bowl and sprinkle with the crushed peanuts and the stir-fried ingredients. Serve warm or cold.

VARIATION

If you don't like particularly spicy food, substitute red (bell) pepper strips for some or all of the chillies.

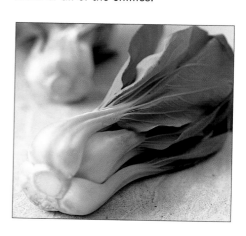

Energy 93Kcal/384kJ; Protein 2.9g; Carbohydrate 6.2g, of which sugars 5.7g; Fat 6.4g, of which saturates 0.9g; Cholesterol 0mg; Calcium 157mg; Fibre 2.1g; Sodium 354mg.

HOT AND SPICY YAM

THE YAM OF THE TITLE ISN'T THE VEGETABLE THAT RESEMBLES SWEET POTATO, BUT IS RATHER A NAME GIVEN TO A SPICY SAUCE BASED ON COCONUT MILK AND MUSHROOMS. IT IS EASY TO MAKE IN THE WOK AND TASTES GOOD WITH STEAMED GREENS, BEANSPROUTS, BEANS AND BROCCOLI.

SERVES FOUR

INGREDIENTS
90g/3½oz Chinese leaves (Chinese cabbage), shredded
90g/3½oz/scant 2 cups beansprouts
90g/3½oz/scant 1 cup green beans, trimmed
90g/3½oz broccoli, preferably the purple sprouting variety, divided into florets
15ml/1 tbsp sesame seeds, toasted
For the yam
60ml/4 tbsp coconut cream
5ml/1 tsp Thai red curry paste
90g/3½oz/1¼ cups oyster mushrooms or field (portabello) mushrooms, sliced
60ml/4 tbsp coconut milk
5ml/1 tsp ground turmeric
5ml/1 tsp thick tamarind juice, made by mixing tamarind paste with warm water
juice of ½ lemon
60ml/4 tbsp light soy sauce
5ml/1 tsp palm sugar (jaggery) or light muscovado (brown) sugar

1 Steam the shredded Chinese leaves, beansprouts, green beans and broccoli separately or blanch them in boiling water for 1 minute per batch. Drain, place in a serving bowl and leave to cool.

2 Make the yam. Pour the coconut cream into a wok or frying pan and heat gently for 2–3 minutes, until it separates. Stir in the red curry paste. Cook over a low heat for 30 seconds.

3 Increase the heat to high and add the mushrooms to the wok or pan. Cook for a further 2–3 minutes.

4 Pour in the coconut milk and add the ground turmeric, tamarind juice, lemon juice, soy sauce and sugar to the wok or pan. Mix thoroughly.

5 Pour the yam mixture over the prepared vegetables in the serving bowl and toss well so they are all coated with the sauce. Sprinkle with the toasted sesame seeds and serve immediately.

COOK'S TIPS
• There's no need to buy coconut cream especially for this dish. Use a carton or can of coconut milk. Skim the cream off the top and cook 60ml/4 tbsp of it before adding the curry paste. Add the measured coconut milk later, as described in the recipe.
• Oyster mushrooms may have fawn, peacock-blue or yellow caps, depending on the variety.

Energy 66Kcal/277kJ; Protein 3.9g; Carbohydrate 6.6g, of which sugars 5.8g; Fat 2.9g, of which saturates 0.5g; Cholesterol 0mg; Calcium 74mg; Fibre 2.4g; Sodium 752mg.

SICHUAN-SPICED AUBERGINE

THIS STRAIGHTFORWARD YET VERSATILE VEGETARIAN DISH CAN BE SERVED HOT, WARM OR COLD, AS THE OCCASION DEMANDS. TOPPED WITH A SPRINKLING OF TOASTED SESAME SEEDS, IT IS EASY TO PREPARE, COOKS QUICKLY IN THE WOK, AND TASTES ABSOLUTELY DELICIOUS.

SERVES FOUR TO SIX

INGREDIENTS
    2 aubergines (eggplants), total weight
      about 600g/1lb 6oz, cut into large
      chunks
    15ml/1 tbsp salt
    5ml/1 tsp chilli powder or to taste
    75–90ml/5–6 tbsp sunflower oil
    15ml/1 tbsp rice wine or
      medium-dry sherry
    100ml/3½fl oz/scant ½ cup water
    75ml/5 tbsp chilli bean sauce
      (see Cook's Tip)
    salt and ground black pepper
    a few toasted sesame seeds,
      to garnish

1 Place the aubergine chunks on a plate, sprinkle them with the salt and leave to stand for 15–20 minutes. Rinse well, drain and dry thoroughly on kitchen paper. Toss the aubergine cubes in the chilli powder.

2 Heat a wok and add the oil. When the oil is hot, add the aubergine chunks, with the rice wine or sherry. Stir constantly until the aubergine chunks start to turn a little brown. Stir in the water, cover the wok and steam for 2–3 minutes. Add the chilli bean sauce and cook for 2 minutes. Season to taste, then spoon on to a serving dish, scatter with sesame seeds and serve.

COOK'S TIP
If you can't get hold of chilli bean sauce, use 15–30ml/1–2 tbsp chilli paste mixed with 2 crushed garlic cloves, 15ml/ 1 tbsp each of dark soy sauce and rice vinegar, and 10ml/2 tsp light soy sauce.

KAN SHAO GREEN BEANS

A PARTICULAR STYLE OF COOKING FROM SICHUAN, KAN SHAO MEANS "DRY-COOKED" — IN OTHER WORDS USING NO STOCK OR WATER. THE SLIM GREEN BEANS AVAILABLE ALL THE YEAR ROUND FROM SUPERMARKETS ARE IDEAL FOR USE IN THIS QUICK AND TASTY RECIPE.

SERVES SIX

INGREDIENTS
    175ml/6fl oz/¾ cup sunflower oil
    450g/1lb fresh green beans, topped,
      tailed and cut in half
    5 × 1cm/2 × ½in piece fresh
      root ginger, peeled and cut
      into matchsticks
    5ml/1 tsp sugar
    10ml/2 tsp light soy sauce
    salt and ground black pepper

VARIATION
This simple recipe works just as well with other fresh green vegetables, such as baby asparagus spears and okra. Vegetables that can be piled on a serving plate look the most dramatic. The sauce gives them a lovely sheen.

1 Heat the oil in a wok. When the oil is very hot and just beginning to smoke, carefully add the beans and fry them, stirring constantly, for 1–2 minutes until they are just tender.

2 Lift out the green beans on to a plate lined with kitchen paper. Using a ladle, carefully remove all but 30ml/2 tbsp oil from the wok.

3 Reheat the remaining oil, add the ginger and stir-fry for a minute or two to flavour the oil.

4 Return the green beans to the wok, stir in the sugar, soy sauce and salt and pepper, and toss together quickly to ensure the beans are well coated. Pile up the glazed beans on a serving plate and serve at once.

Energy 108Kcal/448kJ; Protein 1.5g; Carbohydrate 3.7g, of which sugars 2.2g; Fat 9.6g, of which saturates 1.2g; Cholesterol 0mg; Calcium 13mg; Fibre 2.5g; Sodium 3mg.
Energy 170Kcal/698kJ; Protein 1.5g; Carbohydrate 3.2g, of which sugars 2.6g; Fat 16.9g, of which saturates 2.1g; Cholesterol 0mg; Calcium 28mg; Fibre 1.7g; Sodium 119mg.

SLOW-COOKED SHIITAKE WITH SHOYU

Shiitake cooked slowly are so rich and filling, that some people call them "vegetarian steak". Mushrooms cooked in this manner will keep for several days in the refrigerator, and can be eaten as they are or used to flavour other dishes.

SERVES FOUR

INGREDIENTS
    20 dried shiitake mushrooms
    45ml/3 tbsp vegetable oil
    30ml/2 tbsp shoyu
    25ml/1½ tbsp caster (superfine)
      sugar
    15ml/1 tbsp toasted sesame oil

VARIATION
To make shiitake rice, cut the slow-cooked shiitake into thin strips. Mix with 600g/1lb 6oz/5¼ cups cooked rice and 15ml/1 tbsp finely chopped chives. Serve in individual rice bowls and sprinkle with toasted sesame seeds.

1 Start soaking the dried shiitake the day before. Put them in a large bowl almost full of water. Cover the shiitake with a plate or lid to stop them floating to the surface of the water. Leave to soak overnight.

2 Measure 120ml/4fl oz/½ cup liquid from the bowl. Drain the shiitake into a sieve. Remove and discard the stalks.

3 Heat the oil in a wok or a large pan. Stir-fry the shiitake over a high heat for 5 minutes, stirring continuously.

4 Reduce the heat to the lowest setting, then add the measured liquid, the shoyu and sugar. Cook until there is almost no moisture left, stirring frequently. Add the sesame oil and remove from the heat.

5 Leave to cool, then slice and arrange the shiitake on a large plate.

Energy 133Kcal/553kJ; Protein 1.2g; Carbohydrate 7.4g, of which sugars 7.2g; Fat 11.2g, of which saturates 1.4g; Cholesterol 0mg; Calcium 8mg; Fibre 0.6g; Sodium 537mg.

NEW POTATOES COOKED IN DASHI STOCK

THIS IS A SIMPLE YET SCRUMPTIOUS JAPANESE DISH, INVOLVING LITTLE MORE THAN NEW SEASON'S POTATOES AND ONION COOKED IN DASHI STOCK. AS THE STOCK EVAPORATES, THE ONION BECOMES MELTINGLY SOFT AND CARAMELIZED, MAKING A WONDERFUL SAUCE THAT COATS THE POTATOES.

SERVES FOUR

INGREDIENTS
15ml/1 tbsp toasted sesame oil
1 small onion, thinly sliced
1kg/2¼ lb baby new potatoes, unpeeled
200ml/7fl oz/scant 1 cup second dashi stock, made using water and instant dashi powder
45ml/3 tbsp shoyu

COOK'S TIP
Japanese chefs use toasted sesame oil for its distinctive strong aroma. If the smell is too strong, use a mixture of half sesame and half vegetable oil.

1 Heat the sesame oil in a wok or large pan. Add the onion slices and stir-fry for 30 seconds, then add the potatoes. Stir constantly until all the potatoes are well coated in sesame oil.

2 Pour on the dashi stock and shoyu and reduce the heat to the lowest setting. Cover and cook for 15 minutes, turning the potatoes every 5 minutes so that they are evenly cooked.

3 Uncover the wok or pan for a further 5 minutes to reduce the liquid. If there is already very little liquid remaining, remove the wok or pan from the heat, cover and leave to stand for 5 minutes. Check that the potatoes are cooked, then remove from the heat.

4 Transfer the potatoes and onions to a deep serving bowl. Pour the sauce over the top and serve immediately.

Energy 207Kcal/876kJ; Protein 4.6g; Carbohydrate 41.8g, of which sugars 4.4g; Fat 3.5g, of which saturates 0.7g; Cholesterol 0mg; Calcium 20mg; Fibre 2.7g; Sodium 295mg.

MORNING GLORY WITH FRIED SHALLOTS

Other names for morning glory include water spinach, water convolvulus and swamp cabbage. It is a green leafy vegetable with long jointed stems and arrow-shaped leaves. The stems remain crunchy while the leaves wilt like spinach when cooked.

SERVES FOUR

INGREDIENTS
2 bunches morning glory, total weight
   about 250g/9oz, trimmed and
   coarsely chopped into 2.5cm/
   1in lengths
30ml/2 tbsp vegetable oil
4 shallots, thinly sliced
6 large garlic cloves, thinly sliced
sea salt
1.5ml/¼ tsp dried chilli flakes

VARIATIONS
Use spinach instead of morning glory, or
substitute young spring greens (collards),
sprouting broccoli or Swiss chard.

1 Place the morning glory in a steamer and steam over a pan of boiling water for 30 seconds, until just wilted. If necessary, cook it in batches. Place the leaves in a bowl or spread them out on a large serving plate.

2 Heat the oil in a wok and stir-fry the shallots and garlic over a medium to high heat until golden. Spoon the mixture over the morning glory, sprinkle with a little sea salt and the chilli flakes and serve immediately.

Energy 77Kcal/316kJ; Protein 2.4g; Carbohydrate 3.2g, of which sugars 1.9g; Fat 6.1g, of which saturates 0.7g; Cholesterol 0mg; Calcium 111mg; Fibre 1.8g; Sodium 88mg.

STIR-FRIED PINEAPPLE WITH GINGER

THIS DISH MAKES AN INTERESTING ACCOMPANIMENT TO GRILLED MEAT OR STRONGLY FLAVOURED FISH SUCH AS TUNA OR SWORDFISH. IF THE IDEA SEEMS STRANGE, THINK OF IT AS RESEMBLING A FRESH MANGO CHUTNEY, BUT WITH PINEAPPLE AS THE PRINCIPAL INGREDIENT.

SERVES FOUR

INGREDIENTS

    1 pineapple
    15ml/1 tbsp vegetable oil
    2 garlic cloves, finely chopped
    2 shallots, finely chopped
    5cm/2in piece fresh root ginger,
      peeled and finely shredded
    30ml/2 tbsp light soy sauce
    juice of ½ lime
    1 large fresh red chilli, seeded and
      finely shredded

VARIATION

This also tastes excellent if peaches or nectarines are substituted for the diced pineapple. Use three or four, depending on their size.

1 Trim and peel the pineapple. Cut out the core and dice the flesh.

2 Heat the oil in a wok or frying pan. Stir-fry the garlic and shallots over a medium heat for 2–3 minutes, until golden. Do not let the garlic burn or the dish will taste bitter.

3 Add the pineapple. Stir-fry for about 2 minutes, or until the pineapple cubes start to turn golden on the edges.

4 Add the ginger, soy sauce, lime juice and shredded chilli. Toss together until well mixed. Cook over a low heat for a further 2 minutes, then serve.

Energy 115Kcal/490kJ; Protein 1.2g; Carbohydrate 22g, of which sugars 21.6g; Fat 3.2g, of which saturates 0.3g; Cholesterol 0mg; Calcium 41mg; Fibre 2.6g; Sodium 539mg.

STIR-FRIED CRISPY TOFU

THE ASPARAGUS GROWN IN THE PART OF ASIA WHERE THIS RECIPE ORIGINATED TENDS TO HAVE SLENDER STALKS. LOOK FOR IT IN THAI MARKETS OR SUBSTITUTE THE THIN ASPARAGUS POPULARLY KNOWN AS SPRUE. IF YOU USE THICKER ASPARAGUS, YOU MAY NEED TO COOK IT FOR LONGER.

SERVES TWO

INGREDIENTS

250g/9oz fried tofu cubes
30ml/2 tbsp groundnut (peanut) oil
15ml/1 tbsp Thai green curry paste
30ml/2 tbsp light soy sauce
2 kaffir lime leaves, rolled into
  cylinders and thinly sliced
30ml/2 tbsp granulated sugar
150ml/¼ pint/⅔ cup vegetable stock
250g/9oz Asian asparagus, trimmed
  and sliced into 5cm/2in lengths
30ml/2 tbsp roasted peanuts,
  finely chopped

VARIATION

Substitute slim carrot sticks or broccoli florets for the asparagus.

1 Preheat the grill (broiler) to medium. Place the tofu cubes in a grill pan and grill (broil) for 2–3 minutes, then turn them over and continue to cook until they are crisp and golden brown all over. Watch them carefully; they must not be allowed to burn.

2 Heat the oil in a wok or heavy frying pan. Add the green curry paste and cook over a medium heat, stirring constantly, for 1–2 minutes, until it gives off its aroma.

3 Stir the soy sauce, lime leaves, sugar and vegetable stock into the wok or pan and mix well. Bring to the boil, then reduce the heat to low so that the mixture is just simmering.

4 Add the asparagus and simmer gently for 5 minutes. Meanwhile, chop each piece of tofu into four, then add to the pan with the peanuts.

5 Toss to coat all the ingredients in the sauce, then spoon into a warmed dish and serve immediately.

Energy 287Kcal/1195kJ; Protein 14.3g; Carbohydrate 20.3g, of which sugars 19.5g; Fat 17g, of which saturates 2.1g; Cholesterol 0mg; Calcium 682mg; Fibre 2.2g; Sodium 1075mg.

INDEX